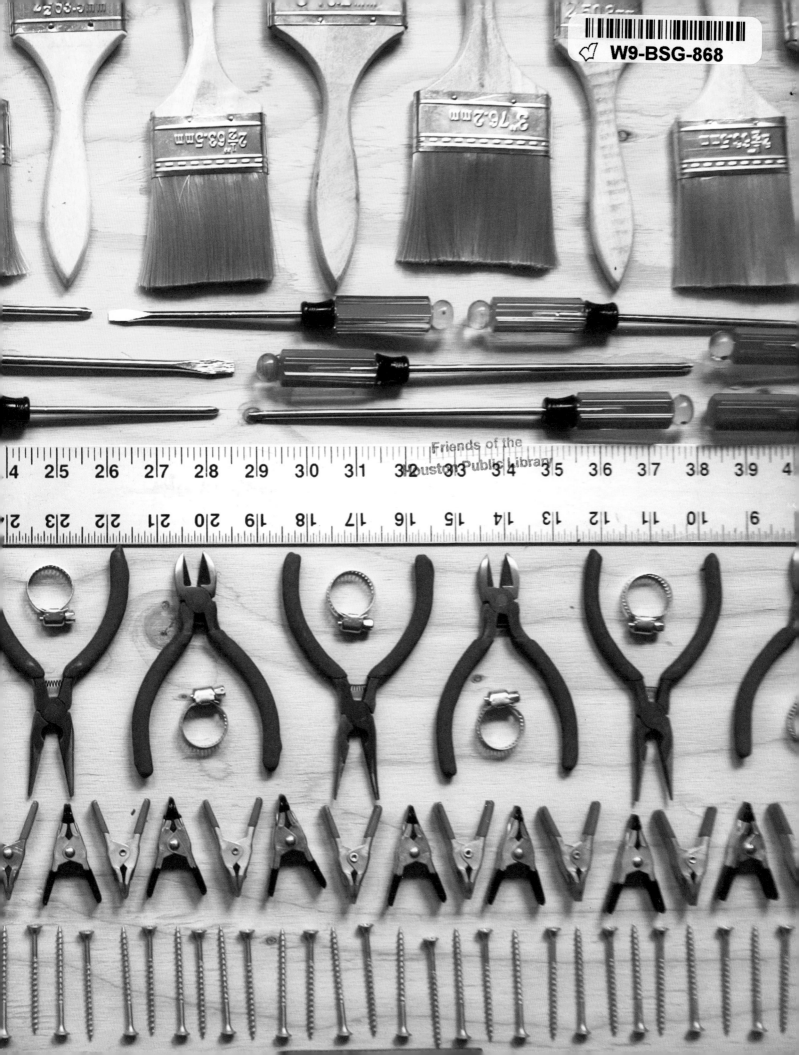

HAND MADE MODERN

MID-CENTURY INSPIRED PROJECTS FOR YOUR HOME

TODD OLDHAM

WITH
JULIA SZABO

ReganBooks
Celebrating Ten Bestselling Years
An Imprint of HarperCollinsPublishers

HarperCollins books may be purchased for educational,
business, or sales promotional use. For information please write:
Special Markets Department, HarperCollins Publishers Inc.,
10 East 53rd Street, New York, NY 10022.

FIRST EDITION

Designer: Todd Oldham

Printed on acid-free paper

Library of Congress Cataloging-in-Publication Data has been applied for.

Images:
© Charles Harper: pages 174–175
Ralph Rapson: pages 144–145
Jack Rosen: pages 56–57
Julius Shulman: pages 50–51, 106–107, 172 © J. Paul Getty Trust.
Used with permission. Julius Shulman Photography Archive, Research
Library at the Getty Research Institute.

Fonts:
Neutraface by House Industries
ERASE by Todd Oldham Studio

ISBN 0-06-059125-0
05 06 07 08 09 ❖/TP 10 9 8 7 6 5 4 3 2 1

MILLIE

LINDA

JACK

Judith Regan

Kurt Andrews
Aliza Fogelson
Michelle Ishay

DEDICATED
WITH LOVE
&
THANKS

Amy Sedaris
Martha Stewart

Murray Moss
Jason Rothenberg
Julia Szabo

Joe Holtzman
Derek Fagerstrom
Vital Vayness

Conn Brattain
Josh Geurtsen
Kelli Hartline

Billy Erb
David Wiseman
John Weigold

Tony Longoria
Hillary Moore
Lauren Smith

A MESSAGE FROM MURRAY MOSS

My very first apartment, in 1969, was in a brownstone on the Upper West Side of Manhattan. I furnished it entirely in found pieces which I "re-worked" on a projectlike basis, painting an elaborate late Victorian armchair kelly green, outfitting an old bureau to become a stereo cabinet, etc. The results were beautiful to me, and the experience so joyous and empowering and memorable, that my first apartment remains—thirty-five years later—my favorite of all my past and present abodes. Through the creative process, it became a happy place to live.

But I wish I had had Todd's book back then!

In *Handmade Modern,* Todd Oldham gracefully and most generously illuminates for us the very spirit of Modernism by guiding us on a visceral, tactile, articulate, elegant, almost subversive tour of the subject, with a glue gun in one hand and a highly informed, sophisticated suggested reading list in the other.

"Making" audaciously replaces "shopping." "Craft" momentarily trumps "industry." For the same reasons we garner more pleasure from our own home-grown tomatoes than from those purchased at our Main Street food emporium, handmade design can be more fresh, more delicious, more nutritious when realized through our own creative, hands-on, and loving toil.

The pleasure of following Todd's artfully communicated, deceptively simple instructions, and then successfully arriving at your completed task, is immeasurable (not to mention the pride you'll have in the beautiful lamp or chair or shelf you've just created!). Take a vacation from yourself: put your charge card aside for just this one moment and pick up your needle and thread. "Modern" isn't all store-bought.

—Murray Moss

CONTENTS

WE can learn a lot from birds; they are nature's own talented decorators and home renovators. This book is a celebration of what our feathered friends do best . . . nesting.

I know, "feathering a nest" is the metaphor most design aficionados prefer. But take the time to look at a bird's nest in its unadorned state. You'll notice it's quite an achievement: cozy and warm, ergonomic and sturdy, despite being constructed with wildly disparate found elements, whether twigs or leaves or—poignantly—paper towels. Some nests display remarkable architectural ingenuity, following all the tenets of great design, naturally. And every one of them is sublimely functional and blissfully unpretentious: the original organic shelter.

I've always admired the modern aesthetic in design. But it's interesting to me how design has strayed so far away from the roots of true modernism, which always combined hand-kissed sensibilities with technology and automation. Sadly, most people have come to think of modernism as cold or sterile or antiseptic or wildly uncomfortable—or all of the above. But it's really not that way at all! Modernism can be every bit as warm and decorative and wonderfully cozy (not to mention unimpeachably pretty) as the most traditional overstuffed bergere—or fully feathered nest.

With this book, we've accented the aspects that keep modernism warm and vital, always emphasizing the *handmade* in Handmade Modern. To that end, we've devised projects of varying "ease levels" that, we hope, will inspire you to use your hands to make your home a reflection of your individuality—not anyone else's. We think you'll enjoy investigating these projects as much as we've enjoyed doing them ourselves. And in the process, we hope you'll feel empowered to devise a few handmade modern projects of your own.

As you'll see, we're not out to create a radical new aesthetic here; we're merely commemorating tried-and-true principles that have guided designers for some eighty years. As we proceed with our projects, we'll visit with some Handmade Modern legends you're probably already on a first-name basis with—Alexander Girard and Florence Knoll, to name just two—plus a few undersung greats who may be a revelation to you, including one of my heroes, the artist Charles Harper.

Maybe you don't think of yourself as being "handy"; maybe you don't yet own all the tools these projects require. But if you've picked up this book, chances are you've already got the best equipment, because imagination and curiosity are really all that's needed for feathering a Handmade Modern habitat. We offer step-by-step instructions for the projects and we encourage you to improvise and adapt to make them your very own.

Good luck to you and happy nesting!

TOOL BOX BASICS

Hammer
Flat Head Screwdriver
Phillips Head Screwdriver
Pliers
Metal Snips

Drill
Drill Bit Set
1 3/4" self-feed Forstner Drill Bit
3" diameter Hole Saw Bit
3/4" Paddle Bit
11/16" Paddle Bit
Screw tips—Flat and Phillips

Jigsaw
Circular Saw
Chop Saw
Hand Saw

Staple Gun
1/4" and 1/2" Staples

Sandpaper in a variety of grits
Pad Sander
Wet/Dry Sandpaper (50 grit,
150 grit, 600 grit)
Tack Cloth
Pad Brush

Paint Brushes in various sizes
Foam Brushes in various sizes
Small Artist Brush
Painter's Tape
Paint Tray and Liner

Respirator/Dust Masks
Drop Cloth
Rags
Clamps
Putty Knife

Screws:
³⁄₄" drywall
1 ¹⁄₄" drywall
Pan Head
Flat Head

Nails:
1 ¼" Finishing Nails
¾" Finishing Nails
Upholstery Tacks

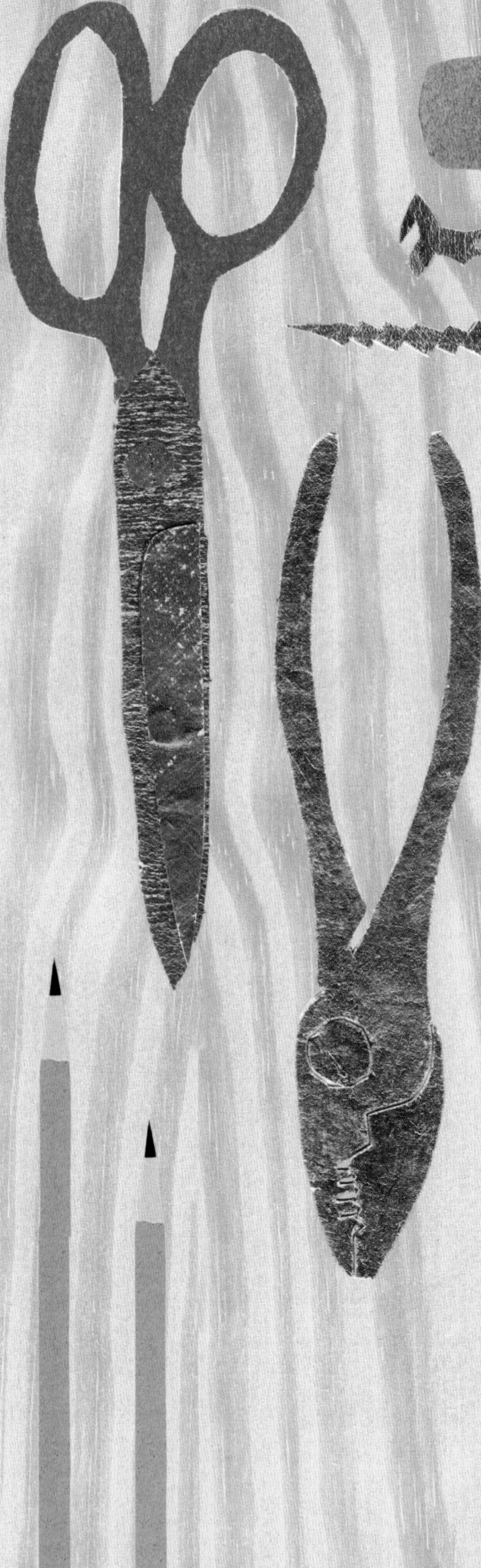

Countersink
Cutting Knife
Rubber Gloves
Speed Square

Tape Measure
Pencils
Chisel
Edge Banding Trimmer
Level
Wood Glue
Liquid Nails

Pushpins
Sewing Machine
Iron
Upholstery Needles
Sewing Needles
Straight Pins

Thread
Scissors
Seam Ripper
Kraft Paper to make patterns

Rulers—Clear and Metal
X-Acto Blade
Self-Healing Cutting Board
Poly-Fil Stuffing

Fabric Glue
FoamFast 74 Spray Adhesive
Hot Glue Gun and Glue Sticks
Mod Podge
Utility Buckets

Plastic Cups
Paper Towels

LIVING ROOM LOUNGE

This cozy living room is the perfect example of a "hodge-podge lodge." Clearly, the components don't technically "go" together—and yet they all blend beautifully. What's more, it's a ridiculously tiny shoebox of a studio apartment, yet this 200-square-foot room feels really spacious. It's in an urban setting, yet the palette is informed by nature: the rich browns of tree bark . . . the sea foams of water . . . beach sand . . . stone gray . . . cloud white . . . sky blue. Here, every inch of vertical and horizontal space is maximized. It's all about solving spatial problems to make a small room feel as big—and as welcoming—as it possibly can: the favorite space to stretch out and relax.

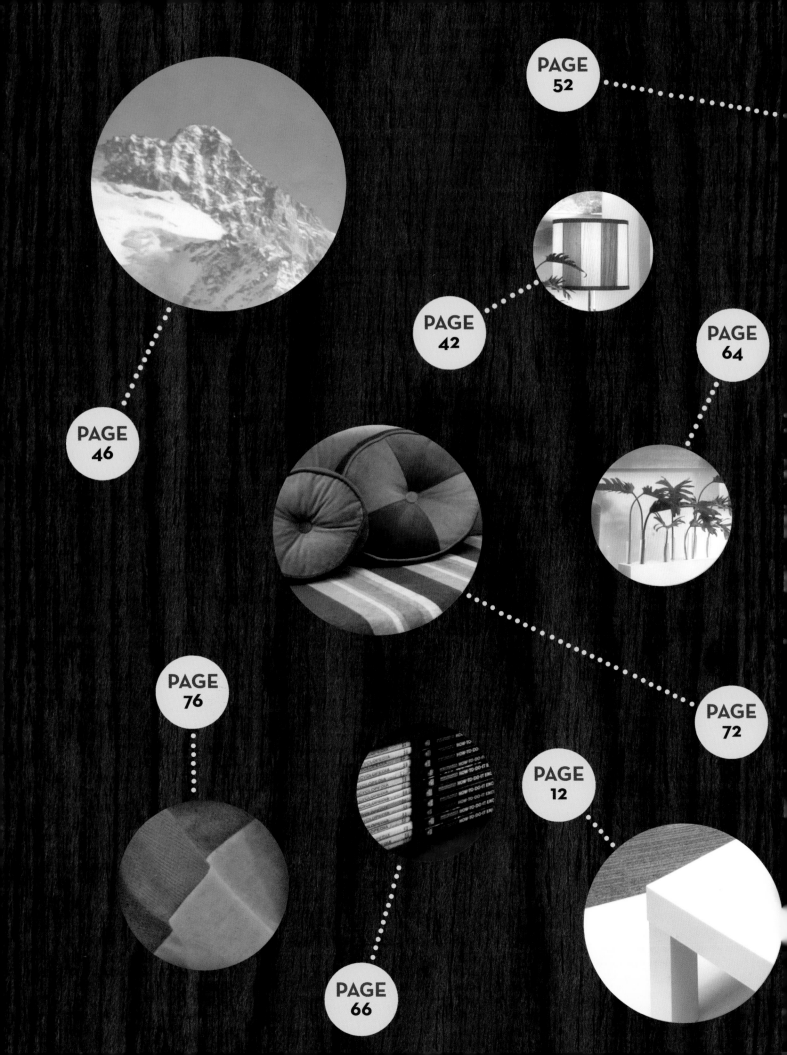

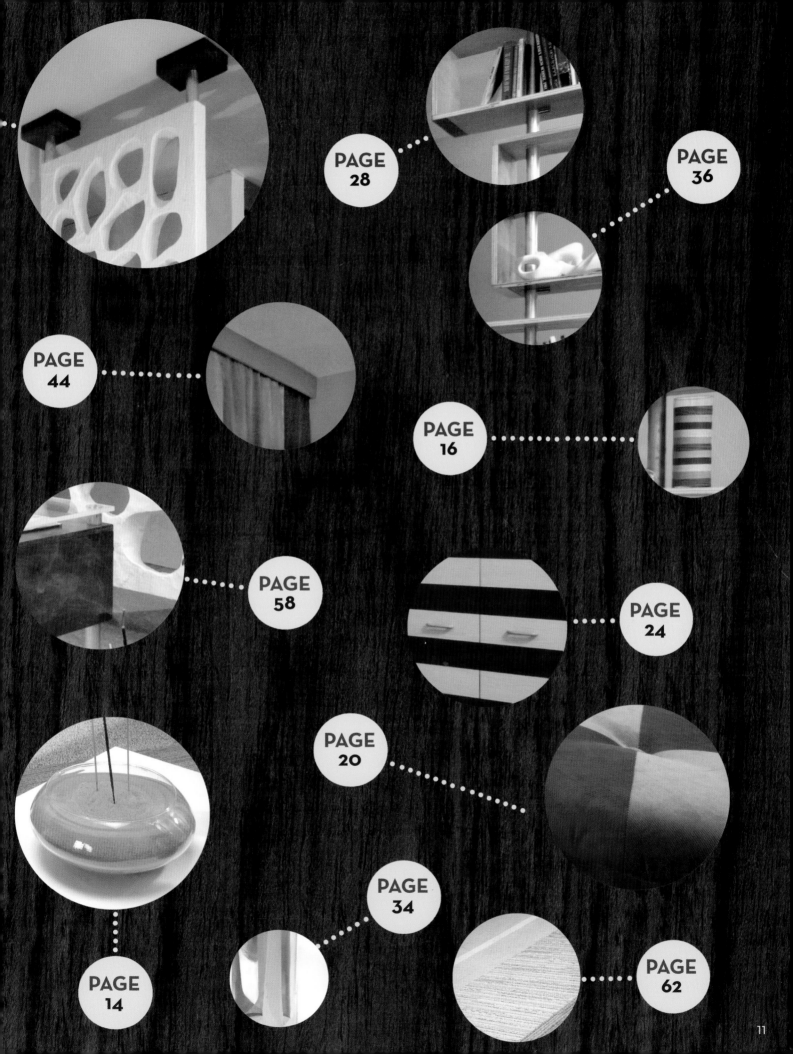

PARSONS TABLE UPDATE

Named after New York City's prestigious Parsons School of Design, the Parsons table is a design icon: a rectangular table with flush surfaces and straight block legs. But don't be intimidated about customizing: even design icons can use a little improvement. By changing the form slightly (sawing off one leg, or all four) and setting two Parsons tables on a diagonal, one perched atop the other, you get a layered architectural look that calls to mind a scale model by Mies van der Rohe—or a drawing by Sol LeWitt.

EASE
1
LEVEL

1 Start with two identical **18" x 18" Parsons tables.** The lower of the two tables will have all four legs shortened. To begin, measure 8" up from the bottom of each leg and mark with a pencil.

2 To make sure that your table sits level, mark all four sides of each leg using a **speed square.** A speed square is the perfect tool with which to mark your right angles, but if you don't have one, try using a folded piece of paper or a magazine.

3 Using a **hacksaw,** carefully saw through each leg, checking your pencil marks on all four sides to ensure a straight cut. Smooth out rough edges of cut legs with **150 grit sand paper.**

4 Only one leg of the upper table will be shortened. To determine how much to cut, place the lower table next to the top table and mark one leg at the same height of the lower table top. Mark all four sides of that leg using your speed square, and cut with a hacksaw. Sand down rough edges with 150 grit sand paper.

13

SAND ART
INCENSE BOWL

Incense brings multi-sensory magic into the home, but incense holders often leave a lot to be desired. This one is practical and as compelling as a canvas by Adolf Gottlieb or Mark Rothko.

EASE
LEVEL
1

1

Pour layers of **colored sand** parfait style into a **glass bowl,** changing colors every inch.

2

For a finishing touch, pour a contrasting color into the center of the bowl to create a large dot. For a chunkier look, use colored aquarium gravel. Or for an earthier feel, try using layers of natural sand and dirt. (See Resources on page 205 for Fred Soll handmade incense.)

Draw pebble shapes onto various shades of self-stick wood veneer. 1

Using scissors or an X-Acto blade cut out shapes inside pencil marks. 2

Peel off backing and apply to clean vase. For top and bottom of vase, cut shapes in half to create a straight edge. 3

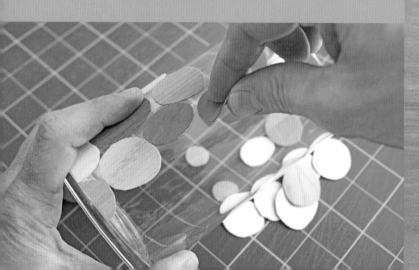

VASE LIFT

Glass vessels adorned with veneer spots or wood-grain Con-Tact Brand paper make the impossible a reality: wood that actually holds water!

EASE
LEVEL
1

1. Using a **straight edge ruler**, measure and mark strips of equal widths on various shades of **wood-grain Con-Tact Brand paper**. To determine the length of your strips measure the circumference of the vase and add ¹/₂" for overlap.

2. Using scissors or an X-Acto blade, cut out strips and begin applying, placing your first strip ¹/₄" up from the bottom of the vase.

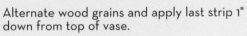

3. Alternate wood grains and apply last strip 1" down from top of vase.

CHARLES AND RAY EAMES

They were the motorcycle-riding, pipe-smoking Mom and Pop of modern American style; the husband-and-wife team of designers who influenced generations and will inspire many more generations to come: Charles and Ray Eames.

The Eameses' furniture designs have such an interesting duality. They are very precisely engineered, yet softened by a wonderful handmade quality. Ray's roots as an artist and sculptor really show in the walnut stools, which echo African sculpture. These bent-plywood chairs are like a magnificent magic trick: hardwood sculptures that are totally inviting. And because these items were—and continue to be—mass-produced, many people could afford to bring them home.

Everything the Eameses created put the "fun" in functional, starting with a leg splint bent out of a single piece of wood, yet lovely enough to hang on the wall as artwork.

Standing on its wire-rod base, the Elliptical table looks like a surfboard ready for action. With its bold color blocks, the Eames Storage Unit, or ESU for short, puts one in mind of kindergarten cubbyholes, making organization an easy game. The Folding Screen undulates like the waves in the ocean. And the Hang-It-All speaks for itself: a wittily named coat rack made of whimsical wooden balls painted in bright colors, like an intricate juggling act freeze-framed on the wall.

I first saw pictures of the couple's California house in magazines in the '70s, when I was a kid. To me, the Eames house looked the closest to the forts I used to build with boxes in my backyard! I still think it's one of the most quintessentially cozy, inviting homes I've ever seen. I wanted to live in it then, and I still do.

What I admire most about Charles and Ray Eames was how multitalented they were, how unafraid to try their hands at new forms of creative expression. Between them, there was little they didn't do: graphic design, drawing, painting, photography, filmmaking. The Eameses were the ultimate poster couple for D.I.Y., and they made it look so easy.

But most of all, their confidence made everyone looking at their designs feel confident too, as if you and I could live with simple, modern style and have a grand good time doing it. From the Eameses and their work, you always get the sense that your taste level is just fine.

New designs arrive on the scene all the time, but the Eameses' work has been around for half a century, and it still looks young. Charles once said he wanted the iconic Lounge Chair to have the "warm, receptive look of a well-used first baseman's mitt." The Eameses' work is forever young because it appeals to the kid in us all.

CORDUROY OTTOMAN

EASE
3
LEVEL

This piece is inspired by the ottomans Alexander Girard designed for Braniff Airways. It's great when guests come over, because several people can put their feet up on it or, with a tray on top, it also functions as a cocktail table. We made it deliberately low to the ground, and gave it a generous seat depth because the action of plopping down on something low and wide automatically signals your body to relax, hang out, and have a good time.

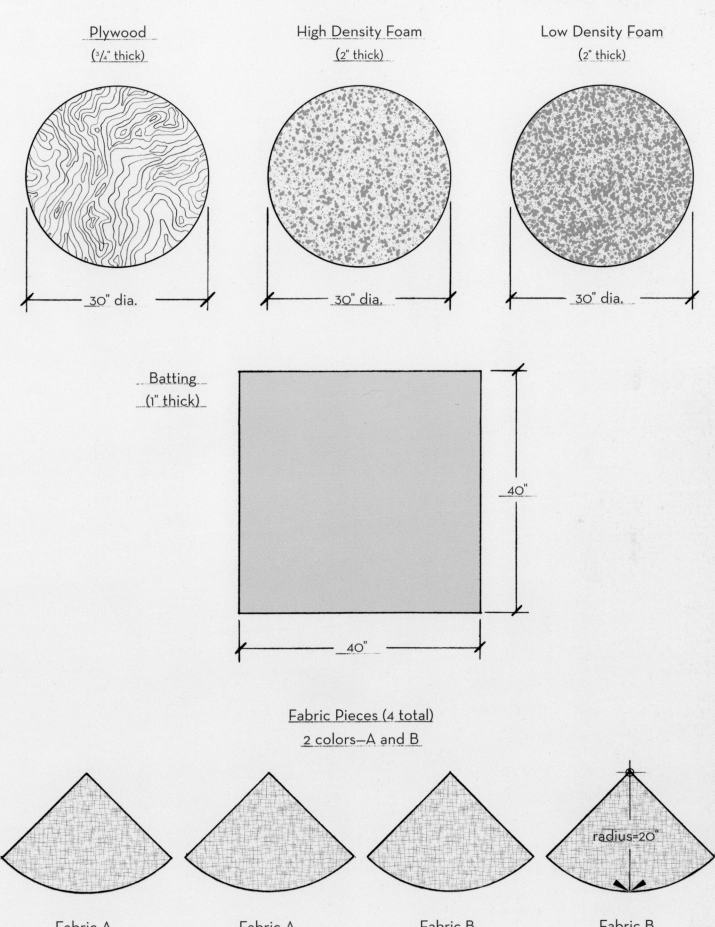

Plywood
(¾" thick)

High Density Foam
(2" thick)

Low Density Foam
(2" thick)

30" dia.

30" dia.

30" dia.

Batting
(1" thick)

40"

40"

Fabric Pieces (4 total)

2 colors—A and B

radius=20"

Fabric A

Fabric A

Fabric B

Fabric B

1 Using your **yardstick** and a **marker,** draw a line 30" long onto your **plywood** piece and mark the center at 15".

2 To mark your circle, create a makeshift compass using a **piece of string** tied around a **pushpin** and secured at the 15" point. Tie marker to other end of string 15" from center point. Keeping string taut, draw the circumference of your circle.

3 Cut out circular piece using a **jigsaw.** Be sure to guide your jigsaw gently—don't force.

4 Stain and seal four **8" wooden legs,** so they will be dry by the time they are ready to be attached.

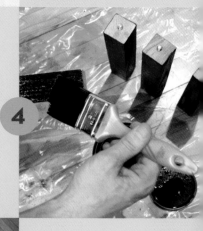

5 Using **FoamFast 74 spray adhesive,** glue **high density foam** to wooden base.

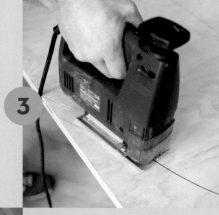

6 Apply a light layer of spray adhesive to the top of the high density foam.

7 Attach the **medium density foam** piece to top of high density piece. Using two types of foam allows for extra comfort and support.

8 Place the seat, foam side down, onto a piece of **1" thick batting.**

9 Attach batting with a **staple gun,** pulling taut from opposite sides.

10 Rotate disk one quarter turn, and continue stapling at opposite points.

11 Continue stapling until batting is secure all the way around. Trim off any excess batting, 1/2" away from your staple line.

12 To make your two-tone seat cover, cut out pattern pieces in dimensions noted on blueprint (page 21) and sew as instructed in Round Corduroy Pillow project (page 72; steps 1–8). Lay sewn seat cover face down and center seat cushion face down on top.

13 Staple seat cover to plywood base in same fashion as you attached your batting, pulling taut from opposite sides.

14 Rotate cushion one quarter turn, and continue stapling at opposite points.

15 Continue stapling until seat cover is secured all the way around. Trim off excess corduroy 1" away from your staple line.

16 Cut out a **felt** circle that is 28" in diameter, using the compass method as described in steps 1 and 2. For a finished, clean look, staple felt circle to bottom of ottoman, making sure to hide all raw edges.

17 Line up all four **metal leg brackets** with fabric seams on bottom side of cushion 3" in from outside edge and attach with screws.

18 Screw legs securely into brackets.

19 Cover your **button** as described in Round Corduroy Pillow project (page 72). Place the **washer** onto the **screw** and create a dimple by screwing it through the center of your cushion and about 1/2" into the underlying wood layer.

20 Attach covered button at center of ottoman using your **upholstery needle** and **thread**.

ALL-IN-ONE ROOM DIVIDER

SOFA BENCH

Under a Mondrian-esque grid of shelves, this bench combines seating and storage needs in one stylish design. If you need more shelves, simply eliminate the bench and extend the shelving to the floor.

EASE
5
LEVEL

1

Cut, sand, and stain all wooden pieces as noted in blueprint on page 32. Using a ³/₈" **bit,** drill pilot holes as noted, through a piece of tape to avoid splintering.

2

Attach center support (e) to base (c) using **1 ⁵/₈" drywall screws.**

3

Attach interior panel (d) to center support (e) using 1 ⁵/₈" drywall screws. Make sure center support (e) is at a right angle to both base (c) and interior panel (d).

PART 1

4

Attach sides (a and b) to interior panel (d) and base (c). You have now assembled the skeleton frame for the sofa bench.

5

Using a **speed square,** mark locations onto masking tape for kick blocks (o) on under side of base (c). This will help the pencil line to show up more clearly. Blocks are to be inset 1 ³/₄" in from both sides, in each corner.

6

Each kick block is two pieces thick. Attach the first piece as shown, using **1 ¹/₄" drywall screws.** Attach the second piece, drilling into opposing corners.

7 Attach sides of kick (n) to kick blocks (o). Then, attach face and back of kick (m) to kick blocks (o) and sides (n).

8 Attach seat base (f) to sides (a and b) and center support (e), using 1 5/8" drywall screws, making sure to align carefully before attaching.

TIP

To avoid splintering when drilling, slow down the speed of the drill as the screwhead nears the wood.

9 Attach center shelf (g) to assembly, screwing in through sides (a and b), using 1 5/8" drywall screws. Make sure the shelf is flush with the angled lines on sides (a and b).

10 Place top piece (h) faceup onto a **scrap piece of plywood.** If you have not already done so, drill two pilot holes using a 1/8" bit in top piece (h) at locations specified on blueprint (page 32). Using a **1 3/4" diameter self-feed forstner bit,** drill holes for pipe, as shown.

11 On under side of top piece (h), attach plywood backing to prevent pipe supports for floating boxes from sliding through cabinet, using 1 1/4" drywall screws.

TIP

When using a self-feed forstner bit, drill slowly and don't force it—let the drill do the work.

12 Attach top piece (h) to sides (a and b) using 1 5/8" drywall screws.

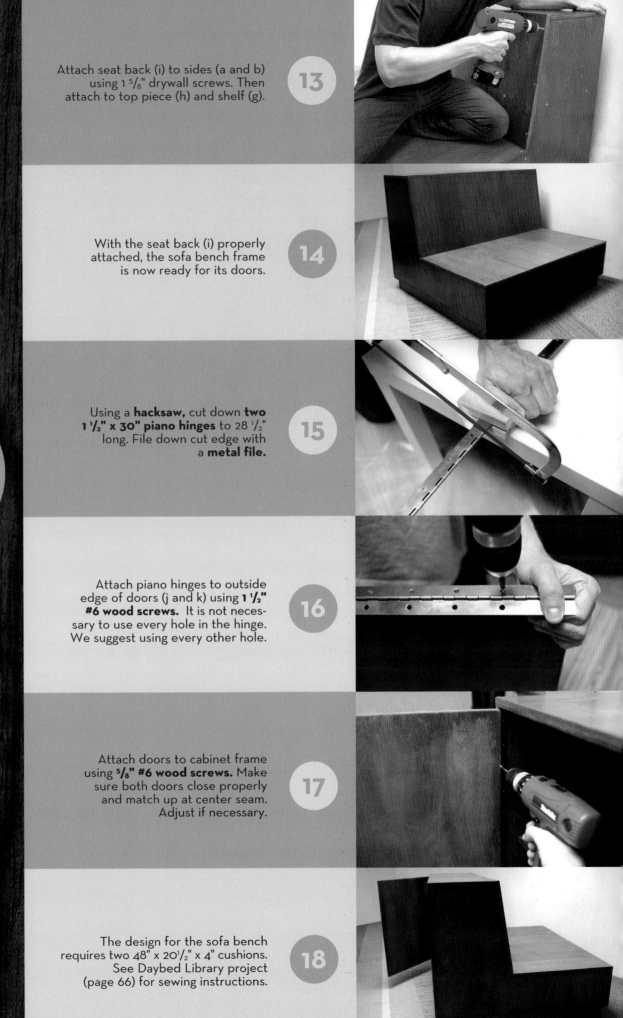

13 Attach seat back (i) to sides (a and b) using 1 ⁵⁄₈" drywall screws. Then attach to top piece (h) and shelf (g).

14 With the seat back (i) properly attached, the sofa bench frame is now ready for its doors.

TIP
To mark cut lines on metal hinges, use removable, low-tack painter's tape instead of a marker or pen.

15 Using a **hacksaw,** cut down **two 1 ¹⁄₂" x 30" piano hinges** to 28 ¹⁄₂" long. File down cut edge with a **metal file.**

16 Attach piano hinges to outside edge of doors (j and k) using **1 ¹⁄₂" #6 wood screws.** It is not necessary to use every hole in the hinge. We suggest using every other hole.

17 Attach doors to cabinet frame using **⁵⁄₈" #6 wood screws.** Make sure both doors close properly and match up at center seam. Adjust if necessary.

18 The design for the sofa bench requires two 48" x 20¹⁄₂" x 4" cushions. See Daybed Library project (page 66) for sewing instructions.

ALL-IN-ONE ROOM DIVIDER

FLOATING BOXES AND TRIM

The back of the bench doubles as a cabinet for even more storage capability—and offers a prime surface for the application of wonderfully decorative wood veneer.

PART 2

1 Cut, predrill, and sand all wood pieces as noted in blueprint.

2 Apply two coats **Burgundy Minwax water-based stain** to wood pieces as noted in blueprint.

3 Using a **soft cotton cloth,** wipe off excess stain.

4 Seal wood using a **pad brush** and **polycrylic satin finish.**

5 To make the wooden supports, cut and stain six pieces of ³/₄" **plywood** into 6" x 6" squares. Stack two sets of two layers each and drill a hole through both layers using a 1 ³/₄" **diameter self-feed forstner drill bit.**

6 Using a **jigsaw,** cut one square from each stack in half. At this point, you should have two groups of each of the pieces shown here.

7 Using a ½" **drill bit**, drill 1 ¾" **conduit pipe** at measurements noted in blueprint. Cut six pieces of ⅜" **aluminum rod** 4" long to make peg supports.

8 Begin assembling stained middle box by screwing top and bottom pieces onto side pieces.

9 Assemble top and bottom boxes using the same method.

10 Line boxes up in order and thread metal pipes through 1 ¾" openings. Cut six metal support pegs, 4" long, out of ½" aluminum rod. Insert rods into ½" drilled holes under boxes.

11 Using appropriate **wall anchors,** attach solid squares to ceiling, 14" apart.

12 Screw half of cut square to the solid square, matching up the outside edges.

TIP
You may use a hacksaw to cut the ½" aluminum rod supports. Use a 60 grit sandpaper to remove any sharp edges.

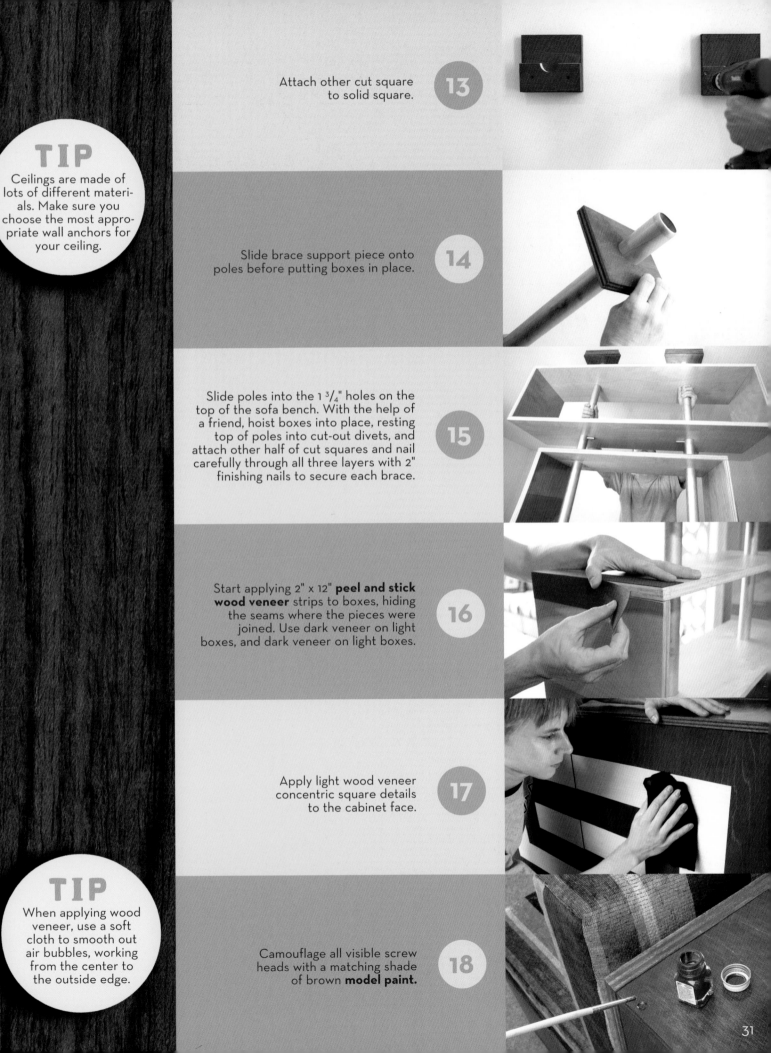

13 Attach other cut square to solid square.

14 Slide brace support piece onto poles before putting boxes in place.

15 Slide poles into the 1 3/4" holes on the top of the sofa bench. With the help of a friend, hoist boxes into place, resting top of poles into cut-out divets, and attach other half of cut squares and nail carefully through all three layers with 2" finishing nails to secure each brace.

16 Start applying 2" x 12" **peel and stick wood veneer** strips to boxes, hiding the seams where the pieces were joined. Use dark veneer on light boxes, and dark veneer on light boxes.

17 Apply light wood veneer concentric square details to the cabinet face.

18 Camouflage all visible screw heads with a matching shade of brown **model paint.**

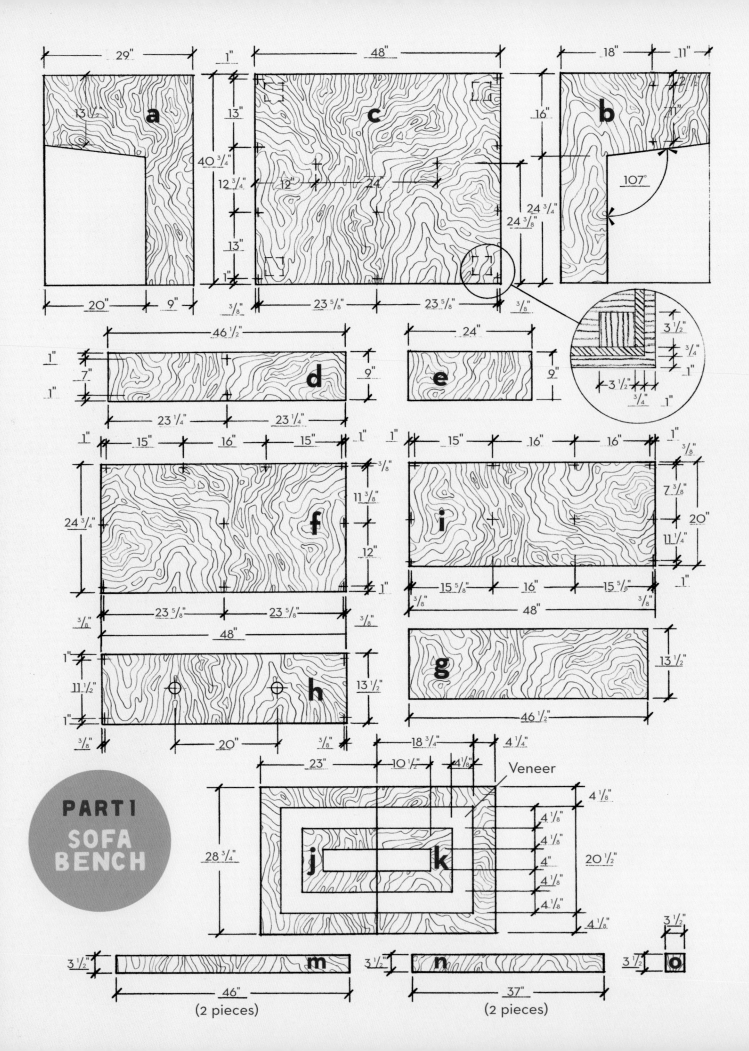

PART 1
SOFA
BENCH

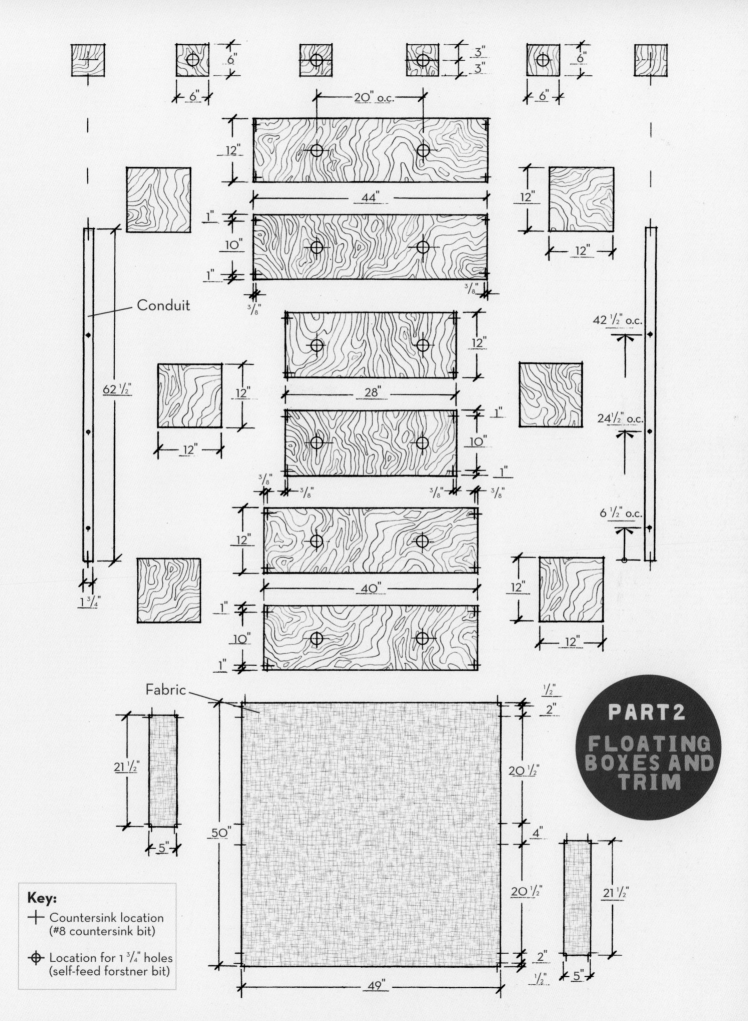

Conduit

62 ½"

1 ¾"

20" o.c.

12"

44"

1"

10"

1"

³⁄₈"   ³⁄₈"

6"

3"
3"

6"

12"

12"

12"

42 ½" o.c.

24 ½" o.c.

6 ½" o.c.

12"

12"

12"

12"

28"

³⁄₈"   ³⁄₈"

1"

10"

1"

³⁄₈"   ³⁄₈"

40"

12"

1"

10"

1"

Fabric

21 ½"

5"

50"

49"

½"
2"

20 ½"

4"

20 ½"

2"
½"

21 ½"

5"

PART 2
FLOATING BOXES AND TRIM

Key:
✛ Countersink location
(#8 countersink bit)

⊕ Location for 1 ¾" holes
(self-feed forstner bit)

33

KALEIDOSCOPE ART GLASS

Hardware store supplies can turn an inexpensive vase into a beautiful work of art: bargain Venini by way of '60s painter Morris Louis.

EASE
LEVEL
2

The two ingredients in **5-minute epoxy** form a strong bond when its two equal parts are mixed. Pour 1 teaspoon of each part into a clean cup and mix thoroughly.

Note: Always work in a well ventilated room and wear a **respirator** when using epoxy.

1

2

Next, pour **denatured alcohol** into the cup 1 teaspoon at a time until it reaches the consistency of thick maple syrup. Add **colored pigment** (we suggest Cast n' Craft color pigment concentrate) to the mix 1 drop at a time. White pigment can be added for more opaque stripes.

Carefully pour mixture into the bottom of your **cylindrical glass vase,** making sure not to drip any on the sides. The mixture cures pretty quickly, so make sure you pour it in while it is still runny.

3

4

Choose where you want your stripe and tilt vase in that direction as you gently pour mix out. Using a clean paper towel, wipe excess color off the lip of your vase.

After your first stripe has dried (about 5 minutes) proceed with other colored stripes.

Consider your art glass a dry vase—water and epoxy don't mix.

5

35

PLASTER MOON ROCK SCULPTURE

One small step, one giant leap . . .
Looking for all the world like authentic
fragments of the lunar landscape, these
objects are made using a primitive
technique, but the end result is that of a
space-age souvenir. Wonderfully sculptural
monuments in miniature, they delight the eye,
evoking the work of Isamu Noguchi.

EASE
3
LEVEL

In a bucket filled with 2 quarts of water, sift in about 4 quarts of dry **plaster of paris** and let sit for 2-3 minutes.

Note: This project should be done in a workroom, garage, or outside.

Mix powder and water with your hands, breaking up any chunks of powder until smooth. If necessary, add more water until mixture achieves the consistency of cake batter and will coat your hand like a glove. Mix for 3-5 minutes. Tap the sides of the bucket to release any air bubbles that may have formed during mixing.

Never rinse your hands or containers covered with plaster in the sink. Always have a separate bucket of clean water in which to rinse. Plaster will permanently clog your pipes.

Slowly pour the mix into a **1-gallon milk jug,** with the top 2" cut off. Lightly tap milk jug to dislodge any trapped air bubbles. Wait about 1/2 hour until plaster hardens.

Carefully cut sides of milk jug with a **utility knife** to release plaster.

5 Before you begin sculpting, determine the general shape of your form by making a rough sketch onto your plaster with a pencil. Using a **1" chisel and hammer,** shape the edges and corners until you get a rough version of your final shape. Don't forget to wear a dust mask when you perform this step.

Note: It is easiest to carve the plaster right after it hardens and is still wet. If your plaster has dried too much, you can immerse it in water for 10 minutes.

To create open spaces in your sculpture, drill two or three holes in from various sides and angles, using a **³/₄" paddle bit.** For structural integrity, make sure that you always have a wall thickness of at least 1" around each hole.

6

7 To soften the gouges left by the drill and chisel, start smoothing the surfaces using a **shaper.** Continue refining the form until you are satisfied with the shape.

Continue the smoothing process with **wet/dry sandpaper,** starting with a coarse 50 grit. You can refine it even further by using grits that are higher in number. We suggest moving onto a 150 grit and ending with a 600 grit paper. If your sandpaper gets caked with plaster as you are sanding, you can clean it off by immersing it in water. Finish sculptures with two or three coats of **spray satin polyurethane.**

8

"Everything is sculpture," Isamu Noguchi once said. "Any material, any idea without hindrance born into space, I consider sculpture." He was an artist first and always, but fortunately for us, Noguchi also enjoyed developing bestselling products for Alcoa, Zenith, Steuben, Herman Miller, and Knoll, many of which continue to be produced, still brightening the design landscape.

The most memorable are his glass-topped biomorphic table (designed in 1948 for Herman Miller) and his glorious collection of lamps. No, not lamps or lanterns but "Akari light sculptures," ingenious constructions of paper and wood that arrive folded flat in a box, then pull open and plug in to become illuminated, and illuminating, works of art. What a marvelous magic trick! I get to live with one of these sculptures, a tall, stacked one, and I'm always astonished at its engineering. It's made of seemingly fragile things—paper and matchstick-thin bamboo— yet it holds up beautifully.

For an encore, how about a stool that rocks without tipping over? Or a metal table that resembles a piece of carefully folded paper —solid origami? Noguchi made these too, along with the free-form sofa and ottoman, two of the sexiest pieces of upholstered furniture ever designed. The Isamu Noguchi Garden Museum in Long Island City, New York, displays more than 240 works in a setting created by the artist himself; it's one of my favorite places to visit.

In Noguchi's hands, furnishings became fine artworks that seamlessly blended the aesthetics of East and West (not unlike Noguchi's own half-Japanese, half-American heritage). Normally, we think of artwork as something to hang on the wall or place on a touch-me-not sculpture stand, behind a protective velvet rope. But Noguchi opened our minds to the idea of totally functional art, and how it can exalt everyday life. He literally raised furniture to art, creating sculpture you can sit in, lie back on, read by, even set your drink on. What's more, he proved that art could merge happily with commerce, each enriching the other in surprising ways.

For me, this carries a powerful message: Home is no different from a gallery or museum. It's your own private fantasy art installation, to be used and enjoyed, looked at and touched, not just admired from afar.

ISAMU
NOGUCHI

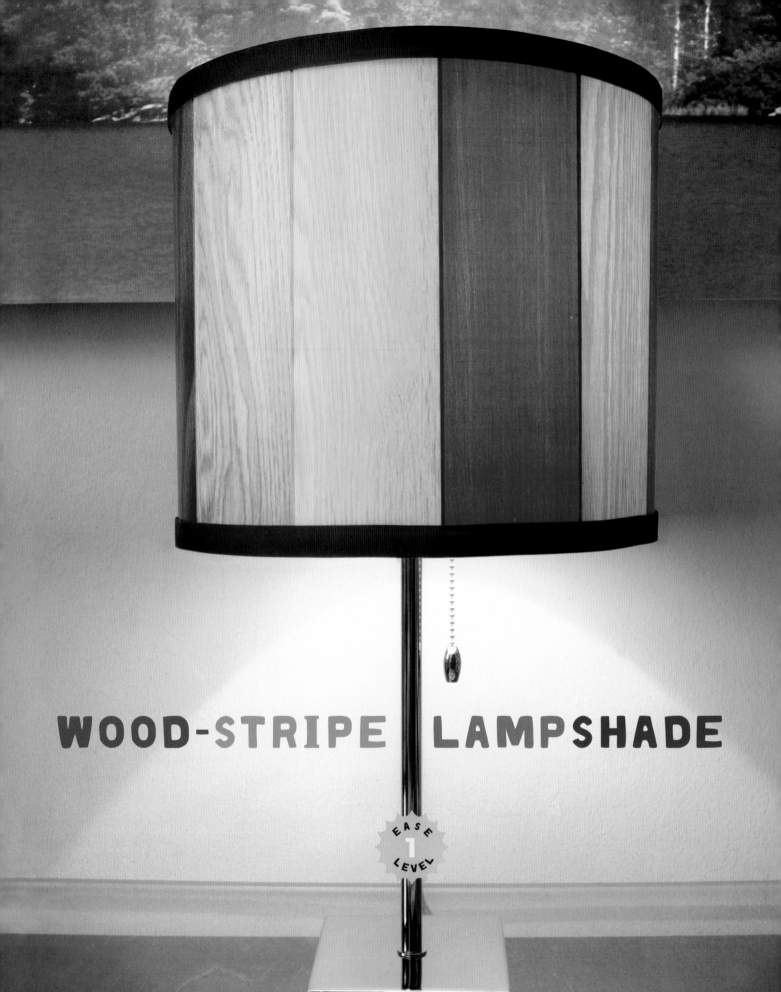

WOOD-STRIPE LAMPSHADE

EASE
1
LEVEL

Thanks to wood-grain Con-Tact Brand paper, this lampshade's
amber glow casts a lovely, flattering light on you and your guests.

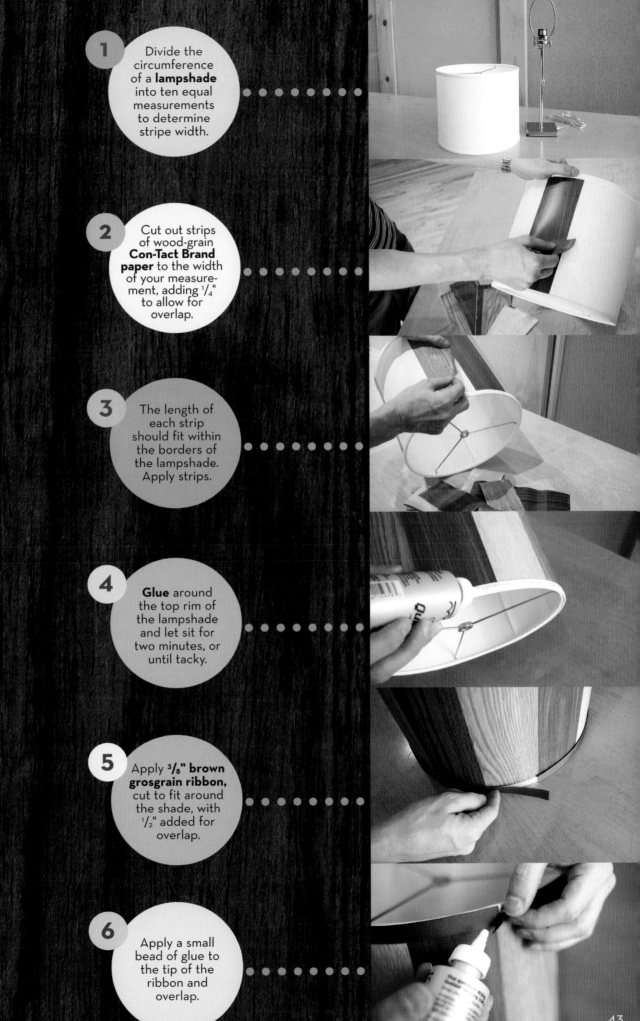

1 Divide the circumference of a **lampshade** into ten equal measurements to determine stripe width.

2 Cut out strips of wood-grain **Con-Tact Brand paper** to the width of your measurement, adding $1/4$" to allow for overlap.

3 The length of each strip should fit within the borders of the lampshade. Apply strips.

4 **Glue** around the top rim of the lampshade and let sit for two minutes, or until tacky.

5 Apply $3/8$" **brown grosgrain ribbon,** cut to fit around the shade, with $1/2$" added for overlap.

6 Apply a small bead of glue to the tip of the ribbon and overlap.

PATCHWORK STRIPE CURTAIN

Custom drapery panels are expensive; off-the-rack curtains are blah. But piece together your own and you can do much more than just cover a window. This vertical stripe panel is easy to make, and hangs with the simplicity of a shower curtain. This curtain successfully camouflages a massive record collection and also gives the illusion of being a pass-through to a whole gallery of other imaginary rooms.

EASE
3
LEVEL

1 Measure the length and width of your opening. To create the two panel patterns needed to make this curtain, divide the overall width in half and add 6" to the length to allow for hemming. Divide the panel width measurement into thirds, determining the widths of the stripes as you wish. Add 2" to the width of each stripe for seam allowance, and cut out.

2 With right sides facing each other sew stripes together with a ½" seam allowance, being careful not to stretch the fabrics as you sew. Repeat for the second panel.

3 To finish raw edges, use the zigzag stitch on your sewing machine, letting the stitch run off the edge of the fabric to seal in the cut edges.

Hem the side pieces with a ½" roll hem. Hem the top of the panel with a 1½" roll hem. After hanging, wait at least 48 hours before hemming the bottom of your curtain to allow the fabric to stretch. Hem the bottom of the curtain with a 3½" roll hem.

4

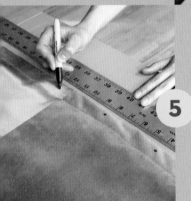

5 Mark grommet holes in the middle of the hem along the top edge, spacing them evenly every 6".

6 Attach **grommets** as instructed on **grommet tool.** Insert **shower curtain hooks** into the grommets and hang curtain on an **adjustable shower curtain tension rod,** 2" down from the ceiling.

For the valence, cut a **1" x 6"** piece of wood to match the width of your opening. Next, cut a piece of fabric that is 16" wide and equal in length to the valence plus an additional 4" on either end. Center under wood and staple, folding up the sides and working from the center out.

7

To finish the ends, wrap the fabric as if you were wrapping a gift, and secure with a **staple gun.**

8

9 To install the valence to the ceiling, attach two **4" L-brackets** to your fabric-covered wood piece, 20" in from each end.

10 All walls and ceilings are constructed differently, so research and use appropriate **wall anchors** for your ceiling. Place the valence 1" in front of the curtain rod and attach to the ceiling with wall anchors at every 16".

INSTANT WINDOW ART

To improve the view in a dark, airless room, let details of '70s photo murals be your permanent vista. Why not look out on the snowy Alps AND a lake simultaneously? There's nothing quite like bending time right in your own living room. But that's not the final frontier: A blow-up of the starry night sky would look pretty amazing, too.

EASE LEVEL 2

47

1 Apply a smooth, even coat of **spray mount** to one side of your **gator board,** holding can 6-8" from the board, and making sure to cover the entire surface. Apply spray mount to the backside of your **poster** and let stand approximately 15 minutes, or until tacky.

2 To attach two glued surfaces together, use a technique called slip-sheeting. The slip sheet won't stick to either surface, as it has no adhesive on it. To do this, use a piece of paper that is slightly larger than your poster as a **separator.** Lay the separator on top of the gator board, 4" from the top edge.

3 Begin attaching the poster to the gator board by lining up the top edges and smoothing from the center out.

4 While pulling the separator sheet down, continue smoothing, using a **piece of cloth** to smooth out any air bubbles. Be careful not to press too hard, or you might dent your gator board.

5 Once you get to the top of the poster, you can safely remove the separator sheet from between the layers. Smooth out any visible air bubbles with your cloth.

6 For a clean, finished edge, use a **utility knife** with a **metal straight edge** to cut through both poster and gator board, trimming the poster to the size you desire.

7 Cut a ³/₄" x ³/₄" **wooden support brace** into two pieces of equal length that are 6" smaller than the width of your poster, in order to give the appearance that it is floating away from the wall. Nail two **#18 brads** 1" from the sides and ¹/₄" from the edge of one of your support braces. This is the brace that will be attached to the top end of your poster.

8 Mark a center line on one of your support braces, as well as on the back of your gator board. Using **white glue,** attach one support brace about 6" from the top edge, making sure to line up the center lines of the brace with the board.

9 Glue bottom brace in same manner as top brace.

10 To hang your instant window art, anchor **eye hooks** into wall using appropriate **wall anchors,** at the same distance apart as the brads on the top support brace. Making sure the openings of the eye hooks are parallel with the ground, slide the brads down into the eye hooks to secure window art to the wall.

CASE STUDY

The Case Study House Program (1945–1966), sponsored by *Arts & Architecture* magazine, was a high point in the history of American architecture—one of very first full-scale efforts by sophisticated designers aimed directly at the masses. Gearing up for the postwar building boom, the program oversaw the design of 36 prototype homes, mid-century modern residences that could be constructed easily and cheaply. The plans were drafted by such legendary master builders as Richard Neutra, Eero Saarinen, Charles and Ray Eames, Pierre Koenig, and John Lautner.

It was the ultimate realization of a Bauhaus ideal that just because something is inexpensive doesn't mean it shouldn't have real design value. And the Case Study Houses proved beyond a doubt that budget living could, in fact, have style to spare, a concept I've always related to.

I also just love the houses, because they made edgy, experimental living look like the most comfortable, inviting thing in the world. My favorite is Koenig's Case Study House #21 (1958). It looked like a time capsule—all sharp angles and optimism.

Today, more than half a century later, the Case Study Program's pioneering concept of bringing high style to the widest possible audience in an affordable package—with no compromise of design—is still genuinely radical. To me, the Case Study Program was a precursor for Habitat for Humanity, only with designer blueprints.

The designs did exactly what they were intended to do: redefine the idea of the modern home. The Case Study Houses had a major impact on architecture both in America and abroad, and even today they continue to fire the imagination of architects and designers all over the world. These are not retro homes; they're every bit as exciting and contemporary now as they were half a century ago.

KNOCK-OUT
ROOM
DIVIDER

If the Flintstones had moved to Mars, the gate outside their cave might have looked like this. A celebration of grouting technique, it's essentially a traditional rock wall with the stones removed—perfect for a prehistoric spaceship, and excellent for defining space in a non-confining, "peekaboo" way.

EASE
LEVEL
5

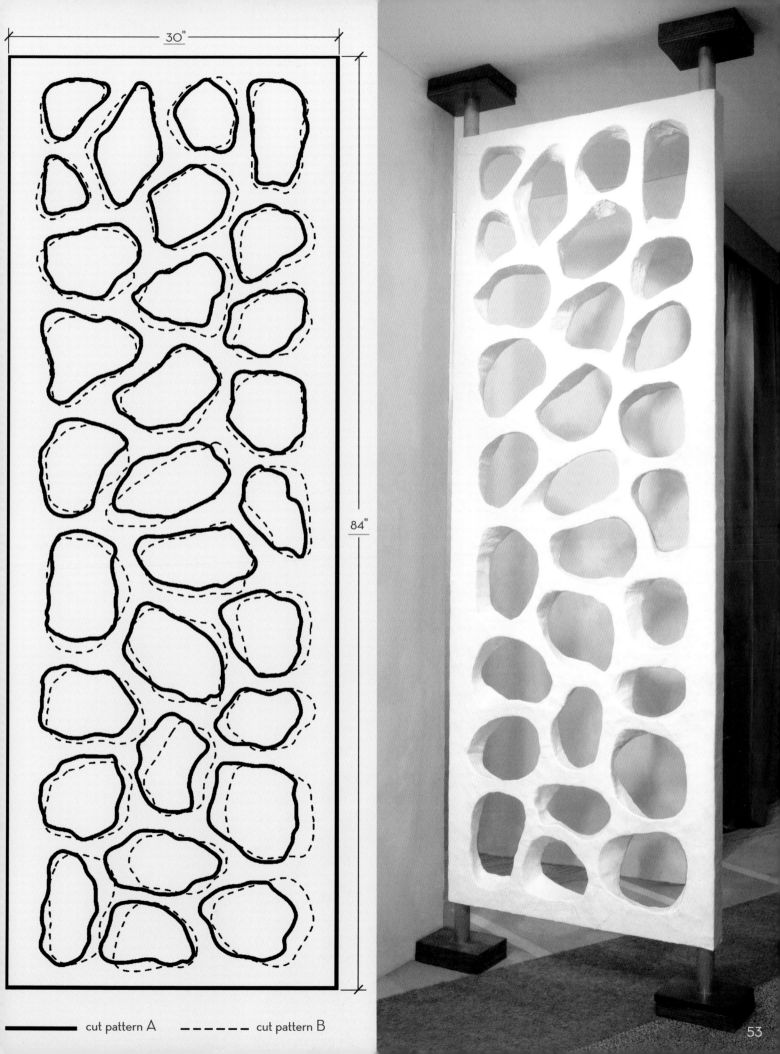

30"

84"

cut pattern A — — — — — cut pattern B

1

Draw a 84" by 30" rectangle onto **kraft paper.** Freehand the stone shapes (see opaque line on blueprint) staying 2" from the outside edge.

2

Next, draw another 84" x 30" rectangle onto **tracing paper** and line up on top of your first drawing. While mimicking the form of the first stone drawings, shift slightly in all directions, no more than 2" past the original stone shape (see dotted line on blueprint).

3

Tape each pattern to two separate pieces of ³/₈" **AC plywood** that has been precut to 84" x 30". Cut out each stone shape with a **Rotozip** or a **jigsaw.**

4

The room divider is held in place with **1 ³/₄" conduit pipes** and wooden braces. To determine pipe length, measure from floor to ceiling subtracting 2" to account for wood braces. Sandwich pipes between cut-outs on either side and attach with self-tapping screws.

5

To add support between the two layers of wood, intermittently attach **1" x 1" x 1 ³/₄" wooden support pieces** with screws.

6

Moisten 18" strips of **plaster cloth** in a bucket of water.

Plaster is messy, so make sure to protect your floors and walls with a drop cloth.

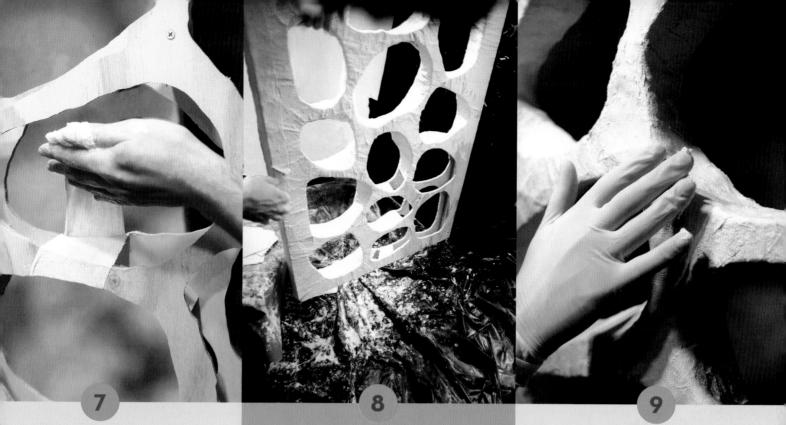

7

Passing the plaster cloth through the stone-shaped openings and around both layers, wrap the entire structure cast-style.

8

Continue wrapping outside edges and all stones until all gaps are completely sealed.

9

Wearing rubber gloves, spread a thin layer of vinyl spackle over the entire structure. This technique will smooth out any rough surfaces created by the plaster cloth.

To make the supports, cut 12 pieces of **3/4" plywood** into 6" x 6" squares and stain. Set four squares aside, and stack the remaining eight into four sets of two layers each. Drill a hole through both layers using a **1 3/4" self-feed forstner drill bit.**

Using a jigsaw, cut one square from each of the four stacks in half. At this point, you should have four groups of each of the pieces shown below. Attach solid square to ceiling with **wall anchors** and screw half of middle square to the solid square.

Repeat on floor braces, making sure they line up with ceiling braces. Slide squares with holes down onto all four pipe ends and hoist wall unit into place, resting tops of poles into half circles. Slide other half of middle squares into place, and nail through all three layers to secure.

10

11

12

GEORGE NAKASHIMA

Visitors to Pennsylvania's Bucks County can make an appointment to tour a woodworking studio that proudly carries forth the legacy of one of America's great designers: George Nakashima.

Though he trained as an architect, Nakashima preferred a more humble title: woodworker. In his hands, wood did not morph into characterless lumber; instead, he left wood alone so it retained all the wonderful, organic qualities of raw timber, including bold sap streaks that put one in mind of a gorgeous abstract canvas. Nakashima used monumental slabs of American black walnut to create tables, benches, stools, and headboards. He didn't "civilize" or try to tame them; he respected their primal, natural forms.

I admire his ability to look at material in its natural state and work around it. Nakashima tailored his designs to complement the wood. Yet the legs on these pieces are so finely tuned, yielding furnishings that combine the elegance of fine cabinetmaking with the sturdiness of a tree-stump. Even his more "refined" pieces retain a wonderful, natural quality; I especially love the three-legged chairs and triangular tables. But whether formidable in appearance or more fragile-looking, every Nakashima design is a glorious celebration of wood.

For Nakashima, design was about honoring the noble trees that supplied the material for his craft. In his book *The Soul of a Tree: A Woodworker's Reflections*, he explained that his goal was to "create an object of utility to man and, if nature smiles, an object of lasting beauty." George Nakashima made nature smile.

ILLUMINATED END TABLE

EASE LEVEL 4

At once a light source, a display case, and an end table, this is truly a versatile hybrid.

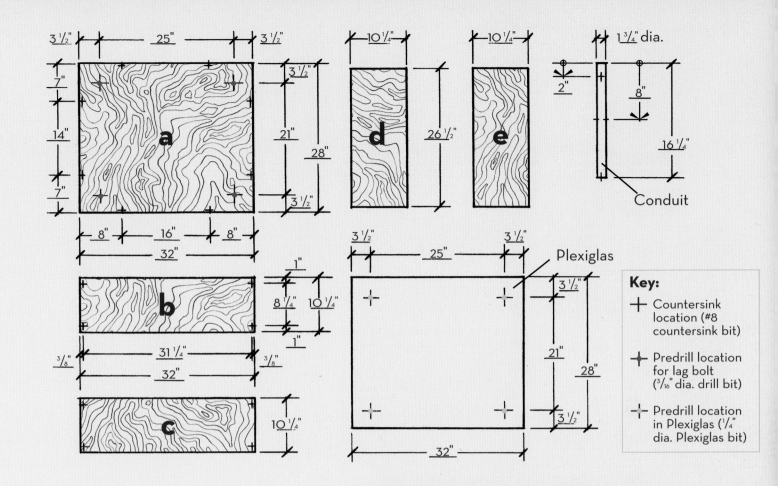

Key:

+ Countersink location (#8 countersink bit)

✛ Predrill location for lag bolt (³/₁₆" dia. drill bit)

✛ Predrill location in Plexiglas (¹/₄" dia. Plexiglas bit)

Conduit

Plexiglas

Have **1 ³/₄" conduit legs,** spacers and **plywood** cut to size. Sand all plywood pieces with **150 grit sandpaper** and **stain.** Finish with **polyurethane,** sand with **400 grit sandpaper** and recoat. Predrill holes as noted in blueprint.

1

2 Screw top piece (a) to front panel (b) with **1 ³/₄" drywall screws.**

3 Screw sides (d and e) to front (b) and top (a) using 1 ³/₄" screws.

4 Screw back piece (c) to sides (d and e) and top (a), using 1 ³/₄" screws.

5 Drill two sets of holes in each leg for attaching to cabinet frame. Holes should be ¹/₈" diameter and perpendicular to each other. The first hole should be 2" down from top and the second hole should be 8" from top.

6 Insert **2 ¹/₄" drywall screws** through predrilled holes in all legs.

7 Attach legs in each corner.

8 At this point in the assembly, your end table should stand on its own, and now you're ready to attach the Plexiglas top.

TIP

Drilling through conduit not as difficult as it may seem. Be sure to hold conduit firmly when drilling, and place on wooden supports to avoi damaging your work surface.

TIP

Glass cleaners will damage the soft surface of Plexiglas. Instead, clean with Plexiglas cleaner or a diluted mix of vinegar and water.

9 To avoid splintering, drill holes for bolt assembly through a piece of **painter's tape.** Holes should be ¼" diameter and 3 ½" from both edges.

10 With protective cover still on Plexiglas, drill ¼" diameter holes in each corner. Holes should be 3 ½" from outside edges.

11 Place a ¼" x 1 ½" **fender washer** inside of conduit spacers. Align with ¼" diameter holes at corners. Place larger ⁵⁄₁₆" x 2" **fender washer** on top of spacer and align with washer below. Peel protective paper off underside of Plexiglas.

12 Peel back all four corners of protective paper on top side of Plexiglas. Slide ¼" x 3" **lag bolts** through another fender washer on Plexiglas and then through Plexiglas. Next, place lag bolt through spacer and washer and into plywood. Repeat this for each assembly.

13 Tighten lag bolts using a **ratchet with a ⁷⁄₁₆" socket.**

14 Attach an under-cabinet **fluorescent fixture** to underside of table as instructed on light fixture packaging. Remove remaining protective sheet on top side of Plexiglas.

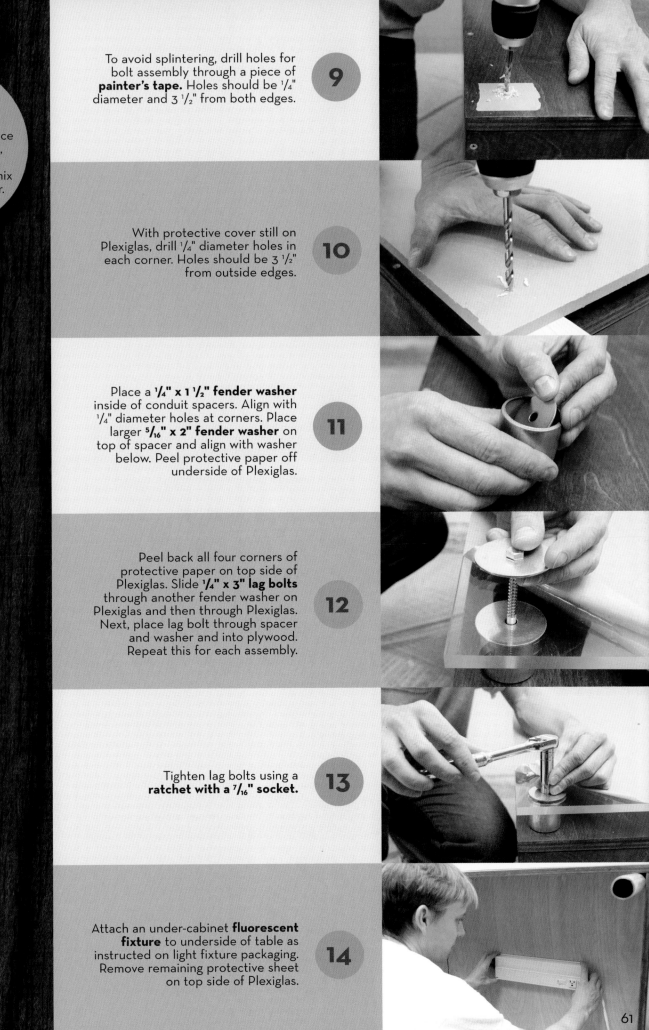

DIAGONAL STRIPE CARPET

Don't be a square: laying any kind of tile "on the diamond" changes the look of a room dramatically, allowing the floor space to stretch beyond it's confining corners and appear measurably larger. Placed on the diagonal, corporate carpet tile gets a downright homey angle.

EASE
3
LEVEL

1

Using **two pushpins** and a long **piece of string,** create a diagonal center line in the middle of the floor from one corner to the other. Begin laying your first stripe of **InterfaceFLOR carpet tiles** along this line, working from the center out and alternating colors of carpet squares for each stripe. Once you reach the walls, you will have to start cutting the squares down so they will fit into the angled spaces.

2

The best way to do this is by creating a pattern using a piece of **brown kraft paper** that is cut to the exact size of one carpet tile. Lay the paper down into the space and create a fold at the intersection of the floor and the wall.

3

Make sure that the direction of your final carpet tile matches what you have laid out in your stripe so far. Lay the folded paper onto the back of the carpet tile and mark your cut line.

4

Very carefully cut your carpet tile using a carpet knife and a straight edged metal ruler and apply the self-stick tile piece to the floor.

Caution: Carpet knives are extremely sharp and should be used with the utmost precaution.

TEST TUBE VASE GARDEN

Flower arranging is a gift, and traditional thinking held that "you either got it or you ain't." No longer: with this eight-step take on the vase, anyone can create memorable, minimalist bouquets with even the humblest of plant matter (flowers not required). Think of it as goof-proof Ikebana or *Kado*, "the way of flowers," the Japanese art of flower arranging that dates back to the sixth century.

EASE
1
LEVEL

1. Mark random placement on a **4" x 4" x 16" wood block** and drill pilot holes with a **1/8" drill bit.**

2. To determine depth of drill holes, place a tape marker onto a **11/16" drill bit,** 3" up from the tip.

3. Drill holes with the 11/16" bit, making sure to hold the drill straight. Sand lightly with **150 grit sandpaper.**

4. Apply three or four coats of **white semi-gloss paint.**

5. Trace shape of base onto 1/4" **white craft foam** and cut to size.

6. Apply **glue** to craft foam.

7. Attach foam to bottom of wood block.

8. Carefully insert **3/4" x 6" glass test tubes** into holes. (See Resoures for test tube supplies.)

DAYBED

This cozy book nook does more than provide a place to rest; it also shelters our reading matter. Think of it as a one-stop reading room—the ultimate bibliophile's hangout.

LIBRARY

MECHANIX ILLUSTRATED HOW-TO-DO-IT ENCYCLOPEDIA
MECHANIX ILLUSTRATED HOW-TO-DO-IT ENCYCLOPEDIA
MECHANIX ILLUSTRATED HOW-TO-DO-IT ENCYCLOPEDIA
MECHANIX ILLUSTRATED HOW-TO-DO-IT ENCYCLOPEDIA
MECHANIX ILLUSTRATED HOW-TO-DO-IT ENCYCLOPEDIA
MECHANIX ILLUSTRATED HOW-TO-DO-IT ENCYCLOPEDIA
MECHANIX ILLUSTRATED HOW-TO-DO-IT ENCYCLOPEDIA
MECHANIX ILLUSTRATED HOW-TO-DO-IT ENCYCLOPEDIA
MECHANIX ILLUSTRATED HOW-TO-DO-IT ENCYCLOPEDIA
MECHANIX ILLUSTRATED HOW-TO-DO-IT ENCYCLOPEDIA

FORTUNE IN A COFFEE CUP

ORBITONES SPOON HARPS & BELLOWPHONES
The Dialogues of Plato
INTERNATIONAL DICTIONARY OF OBSCENITIES   ISBN 0-933394-15-4
The Natural World of the California Indians   California
THE MELANCHOLY DEATH
THE ADVENTURES

Jayne Mansfield and the American Fifties

EASE
LEVEL
4

MECHANIX ILLUSTRATED HOW-TO-DO-IT ENCYCLOPEDIA
MECHANIX ILLUSTRATED HOW-TO-DO-IT ENCYCLOPEDIA
MECHANIX ILLUSTRATED HOW-TO-DO-IT ENCYCLOPEDIA
MECHANIX ILLUSTRATED HOW-TO-DO-IT ENCYCLOPEDIA

1 Cut out **fabric pieces** for back cushion as indicated in blueprint and mark notches as indicated on blueprint (page 70).

2 Fold large piece in half lengthwise with right sides facing and machine baste with long stitches, leaving a 1/2" seam allowance.

3 Press open your seam, and center over a **60" zipper.** Stitch up both sides, 3/8" from the center seam.

4 Using a **seam ripper,** remove machine basted seam to expose zipper. Slide zipper head down, 1" past the cut edge of the fabric and attach end pieces, matching corners to notches marked in step 1. Turn right side out and press seams.

5 Coat one side of your **high density foam** piece with **FoamFast 74 spray adhesive** and place on top of a piece of **1" thick batting** that has been cut to size, matching edges. Spray other side of foam and wrap batting around to secure. Stuff into completed cushion cover.

6 Cover a **2 1/4" button** in matching fabric. Sew through cushion with an **8" upholstery needle,** attaching through a **flat plastic button** on the back side to prevent the thread from tearing through the fabric.

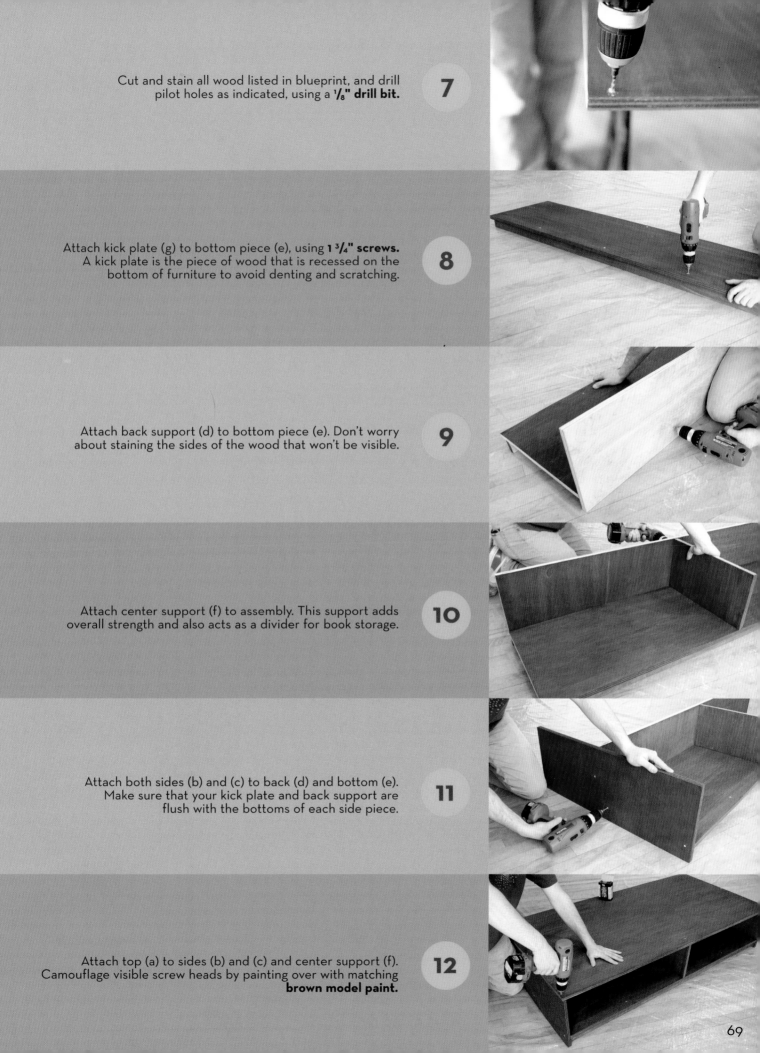

7 Cut and stain all wood listed in blueprint, and drill pilot holes as indicated, using a ⅛" **drill bit.**

8 Attach kick plate (g) to bottom piece (e), using **1 ³/₄" screws.** A kick plate is the piece of wood that is recessed on the bottom of furniture to avoid denting and scratching.

9 Attach back support (d) to bottom piece (e). Don't worry about staining the sides of the wood that won't be visible.

10 Attach center support (f) to assembly. This support adds overall strength and also acts as a divider for book storage.

11 Attach both sides (b) and (c) to back (d) and bottom (e). Make sure that your kick plate and back support are flush with the bottoms of each side piece.

12 Attach top (a) to sides (b) and (c) and center support (f). Camouflage visible screw heads by painting over with matching **brown model paint.**

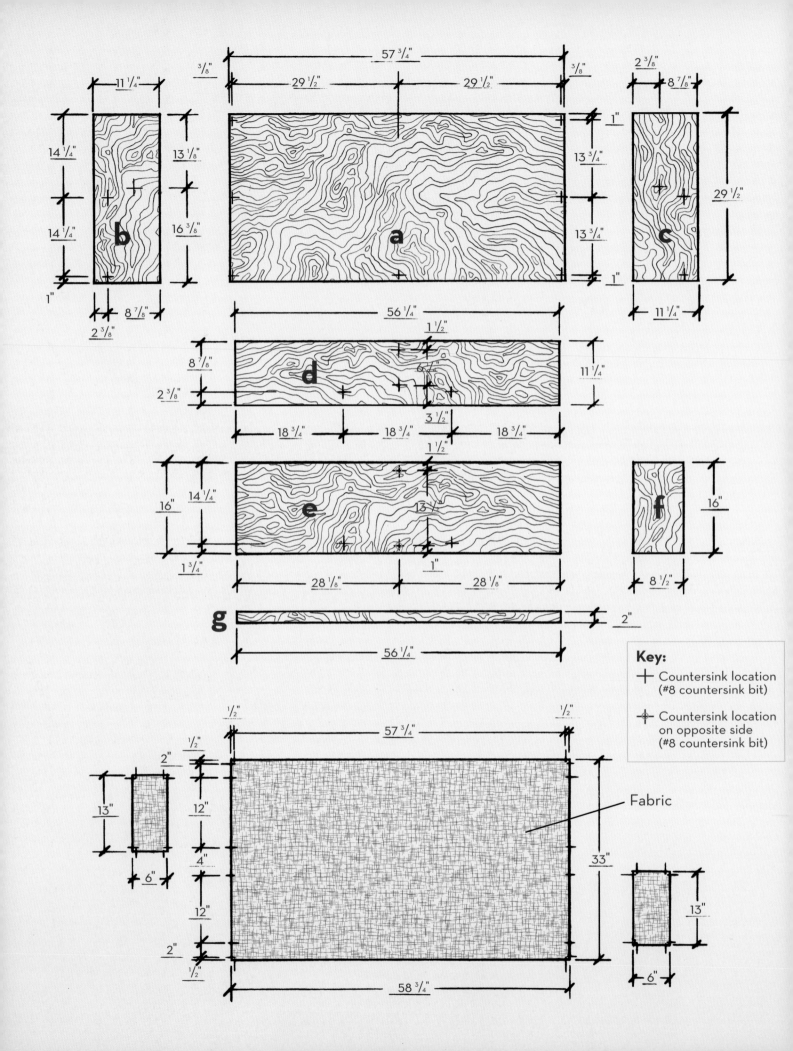

Key:

✛ Countersink location (#8 countersink bit)

✛ Countersink location on opposite side (#8 countersink bit)

Fabric

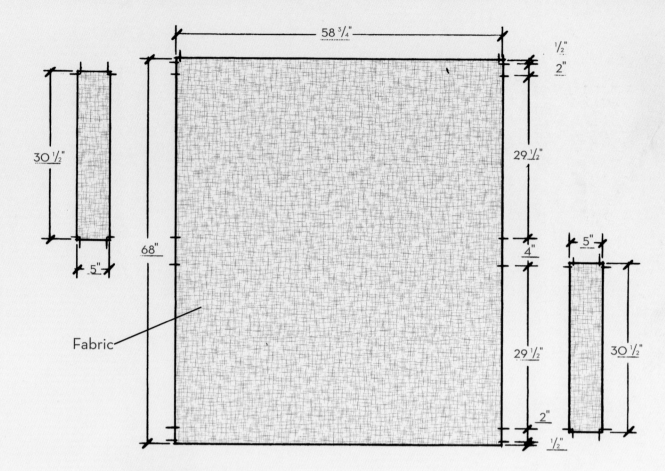

Fabric

SEWING TIPS

Straight seams on zippers are easier to sew with fabrics cut on the straight grain. Fabrics cut on the bias (the diagonal grain) can stretch.

When opening up a basted shut zipper, you may remove the ripped threads with a piece of masking tape.

When sewing long lengths of fabric together, pin the seams together first to stop the fabric from shifting.

ROUND CORDUROY PILLOWS

How's this for a fun geometry lesson: Circles are great for breaking up—and warming up—the cool linear planes of an interior. These cushions are right at home in a modern room, for they manage to be circular and linear at the same time. Corduroy also happens to be the coziest fabric I know; it always looks smart, and it and feels even better with wear.

EASE
2
LEVEL

Directions are for larger, two-tone pillow. Make two **paper** patterns that are 14" square, and fold into quarters. Hold one end of a **piece of string** at the center fold and pull it taut. Tie the other end to the tip of a **pencil** and draw a curved line from one corner to another onto both pieces, creating an arc.

1

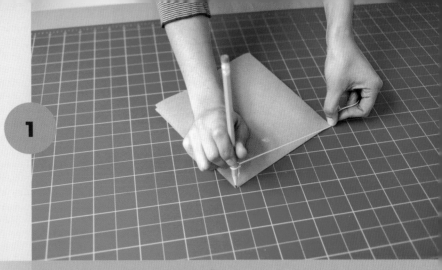

2 Cut along drawn curved line, to create two perfect circles that measure 14" in diameter.

Trace down the fold lines of one circle to create quadrants. Mark your fabric colors, A and B (A=Sage, B=Brown). Cut out quadrants.

3

Mark quadrant pieces onto back (smooth side) of appropriate **colored corduroy**, adding a 1/2" seam allowance all the way around.

4

5 Lay back piece onto fabric. Trace, adding 1/2" seam allowance all the way around the circle.

Cut enough lengths of 1 1/2" bias strips to cover your piping. Bias is a line diagonal to the weave or the grain of the fabric, that will not pucker on curves. You will need 96" of piping total for the front and back edges of the pillow.

6

7 Piece together quadrants for front side of pillow by placing two quadrants of different colors with right sides together. Stitch up one side with a 1/2" seam allowance. Repeat with other two quadrants and press open all seams with a warm **iron.**

Sew each half together with a 1/2" seam allowance, making sure all intersections match.

8

9 Join your bias strips together on the diagonal to avoid bulky seams.

10 Prepare piping by sandwiching ³/₈" **piping rope** in fold of bias strip. Stitch with a **zipper or piping foot,** as close to cord as possible.

With 1 pillow round right side up, match raw edges of piping with raw edges of pillow and sew through all layers using a zipper or piping foot. Repeat on other side of pillow.

11

12 Cut one gusset panel, 4" by 45", out of brown corduroy. Fold in half lengthwise with right sides facing, and stitch along 4" sides, with a ¹/₂" seam allowance. With gusset side down, sew all layers together, using the stitch line of the piping layer as a guide.

Sew gusset to back piece, leaving a 5" opening for stuffing with **Poly-Fil.** Turn right-side out and fill with stuffing in small handfuls.

13

Sew opening shut by hand, and attach covered buttons to both sides in the center of the pillow.

14

To make the smaller pillow, follow same directions, making the pattern 10" instead of 14", and replacing the patchwork side for another solid colored side.

FAUX FUR
COZY BLANKET

This throw is a pastiche of ideas, inspired by an old lady's favorite faux mink, a baby's cuddlesome security blankie, and a teenager's penchant for bold, colorful patchwork. The inspiration was the heavy, utilitarian blankets thrown over the knees on chilly horse-drawn carriage rides, but this version has the chic of après-ski at Klosters, circa 1965. Schuss!

EASE
LEVEL
3

1 Measure and cut out six strips of **mixed fabrics** 12" x 48". Sew strips together with a ½" seam allowance.

2 Press seams and lay sewn panel on top of 2 yards **faux fur** and trim fur to same size.

3 Attach striped panel to fur by edge stitching with wrong sides together.

4 Cut four pieces of **satin blanket trim,** two at 50 ½" and two at 68". Fold in cut edge and trim at fold line.

5 Open trim and place short piece on top of long piece. Sew cut ends together. Repeat all the way around.

6 Unfold satin trim and edge stitch to the pieced side of the blanket, 1 ½" from cut edge.

7 Refold edging and sew to fur side of blanket, using a zigzag stitch and sewing through all layers of fabric.

SWEET DREAMS SUITE

We spend a significant portion of our lives—about one third—asleep, so I think it pays to spend a few waking hours on bedroom beautification. It's all about making our chambers a real sanctuary, and a reflection of personal style. After all, the bedroom is the last thing we see before falling asleep, and the first thing to greet us when we awaken. It's the most personal room in the home, so we want to look and feel our best there. Handmade Modern furnishings and flattering atmospheric lighting help achieve that dream. This is a bedroom environment that's easy on the eyes, whether they're open or shut!

BEAUTY STATION

EASE
LEVEL
3

A modern, substance-meets-style take on the classic vanity table, this features three 2 ½" holes that securely hold anodized aluminum drinking glasses, an ingenious and decorative way to store hair and makeup brushes.

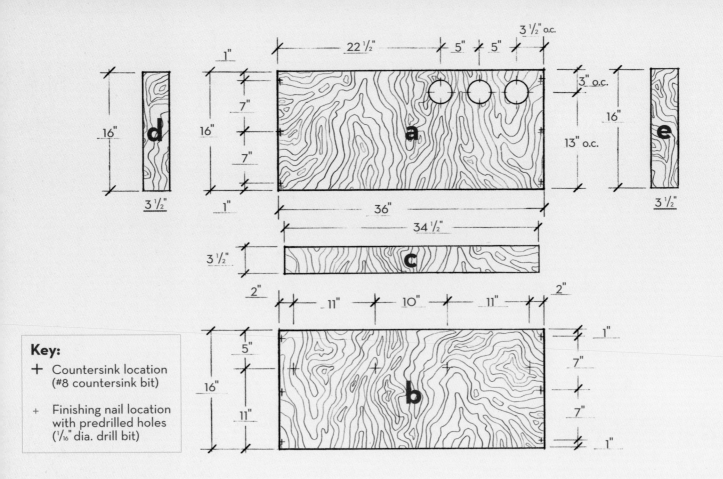

Key:

+ Countersink location
  (#8 countersink bit)

+ Finishing nail location
  with predrilled holes
  (1/16" dia. drill bit)

1 Precut plywood to size. Smooth rough edges with **120 grit sandpaper,** being careful not to round the edges. Apply **iron-on wood veneer banding** to all visible edges.

2 For a clean finished edge, trim off excess veneer with an **edge banding trimmer.**

3 Lightly sand all surfaces with **220 grit sandpaper** and wipe down with a **tack cloth.** Stain all legs and visible surfaces with **water based stain,** following instructions on can.

4 Seal all stained surfaces using a **pad brush** with **water-based polyurethane.** Do a light final smoothing with **320 grit sandpaper.** Wipe down with tack cloth.

5 Predrill holes for screws and finishing nails as outlined on blueprint page. Attach base (b) to center support/back panel (c) using wood screws.

6 Next, attach sides (d and e) to base (b) by screwing through the base piece (b). Using finishing nails attach sides (d and e) to center support/back panel (c).

7 Apply **glue** to top edge of center support and sides.

8 Carefully place top piece onto glued surfaces and attach using finishing nails. Be sure to set assembled piece on a flat surface while drying.

9 Mark locations where holes for cups are to be placed, as noted on blueprint. Cover area to be drilled with **masking tape** to avoid splintering. With a scrap piece of wood underneath, drill pilot holes in top piece (a) using a ¼" diameter **high speed drill bit.**

10 Next, using a **3" diameter hole saw bit,** drill holes at pilot holes. Clean out holes periodically as sawdust will build up and make it difficult to drill.

11 Clean up any splinters using 320 grit sandpaper.

12 Attach tilted leg brackets 3 ½" from face and 6" in from the outside edges, using ½" **wood screws.**

13 Attach **26" tapered wooden legs** using angle attachments. Thread legs into brackets, making sure to tighten firmly. Turn assembly right-side up.

14 Place **anodized aluminum cups** into holes and enjoy.

RECYCLED DUVET
PET LOUNGE

EASE
LEVEL
2

Don't give up on that old comforter with the giant coffee stain—fold and stitch it to form the ultimate pet bed. For the cover, miter a striped fabric to create elegant concentric squares. Your cat or small dog will love this cushion all the more because it smells like her favorite person—you!

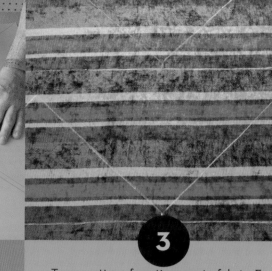

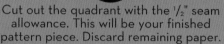

1

ut a 21"x 21" piece of **heavyweight paper** d draw an "x" from corner to corner. On ne quadrant, draw a set of lines that are ½" away from the first.

2

Cut out the quadrant with the ½" seam allowance. This will be your finished pattern piece. Discard remaining paper.

3

Trace pattern four times onto fabric. For striped fabric, alternate pattern direction to create a concentric square when sewn.

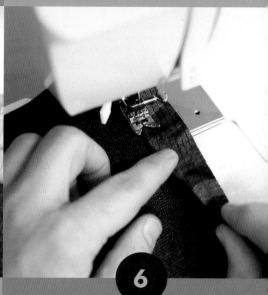

4

ut out two pieces 21" x 19" for the back. You will now have six pieces.

5

Piece together front panel by attaching triangular pieces on angled sides with a ½" seam allowance. Press open seams.

6

To make the envelope back, roll hem 1 ½" up one of the 21" sides. Repeat on other back piece, so hem sides will meet in the middle.

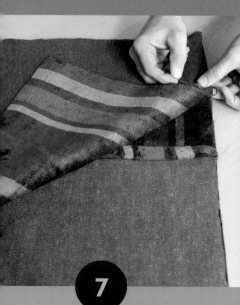

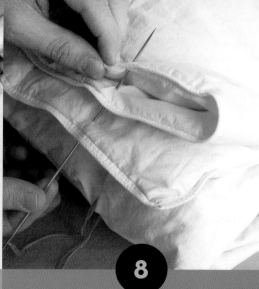

7

Overlap back pieces and pin to pillow front, matching edges and lining up stripes.

8

Fold **duvet** into a 20" square and tack together with embroidery floss so it doesn't come unfolded.

9

Turn pillow case right side out and press seams open. Stuff with folded duvet.

STORAGE BENCH

Pushed up to the foot of the bed, this has three compartments to hold extra bedding, throws, and book-and-magazine overflow from the Bedside Library on page 114. The comfortable high-density foam top is also a great solution for extending the length of your bed, so you and the family dog and/or cat can all enjoy extra leg room.

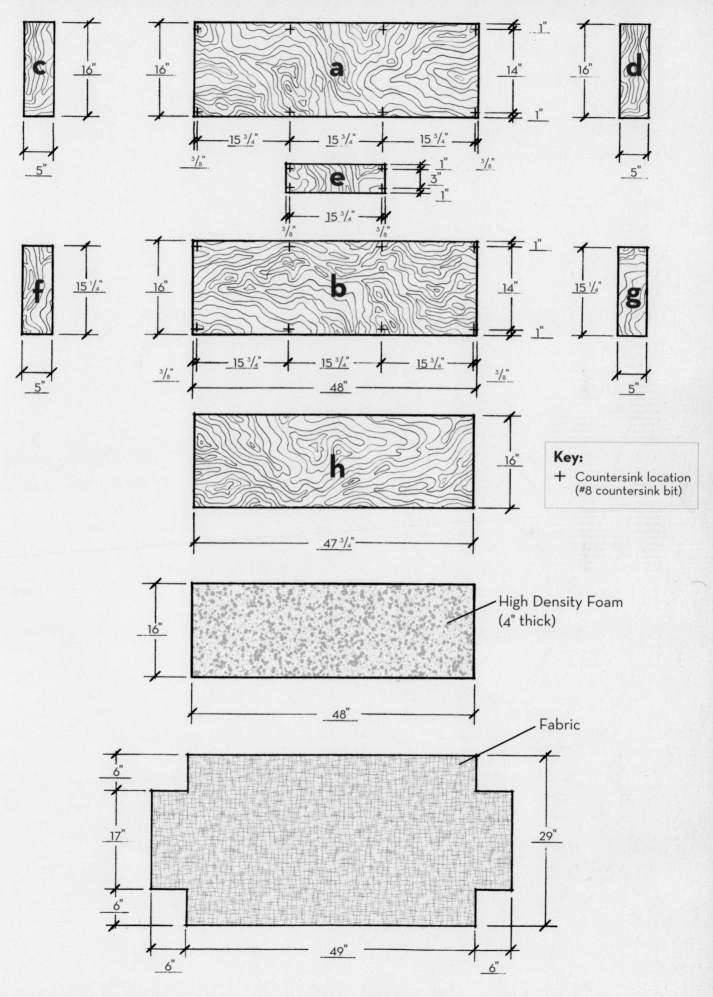

c 16" 5"

a 16" 1" 14" 1" 15 3/4" 15 3/4" 15 3/4" 3/8" 3/8"

d 16" 5"

e 1" 3" 1" 15 3/4" 3/8" 3/8"

f 15 1/4" 5"

b 16" 1" 14" 1" 15 3/4" 15 3/4" 15 3/4" 3/8" 48" 3/8"

g 15 1/4" 5"

h 16" 47 3/4"

Key:
+ Countersink location
(#8 countersink bit)

High Density Foam
(4" thick)
16" 48"

Fabric
6" 17" 6" 29"
6" 49" 6"

91

1 To prepare wood for building, follow steps 1–4 for Beauty Station (page 85) and predrill holes as outlined on blueprint. Attach vertical supports (f and g) to back panel (e) using **1 5/8" drywall screws.**

2 With back (e) and vertical supports (f and g) facing down, attach base piece (b) to assembly using drywall screws.

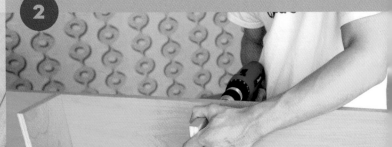

3 Match face edges of sides (c and d) to face edge of base piece (b) and screw into sides through base using drywall screws.

4 Place assembly upright and put a small bead of **wood glue** on top of sides (c and d), interior vertical partitions (f and g) and back (e), for strength. Carefully place top piece (a) on assembly.

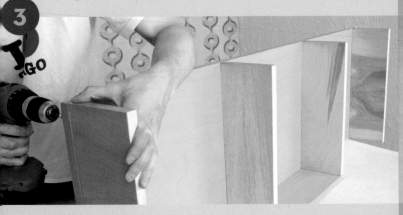

5 Attach top piece (a) using drywall screws. Start at the front and move toward the back to make sure that the top of the face piece is flush with sides and supports.

6 Turn assembled bench base over so it is bottom up. Predrill five holes for attaching the cushion to the base cabinet by drilling at an angle. Space these holes evenly across face.

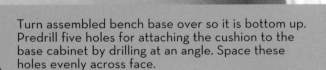

7 Next, predrill holes along the back of top piece (a). Since the back support panel will prevent you from predrilling in the center opening, drill two on either side.

8 With cabinet still face down, attach **angled leg brackets** as shown, 1/4" in from edges, using **5/8" wood screws.** Make sure brackets are angled toward corners.

9 Cut **vinyl** to blueprint specified dimensions and sew the mitered corner seams with a $\frac{1}{2}$" seam allowance.

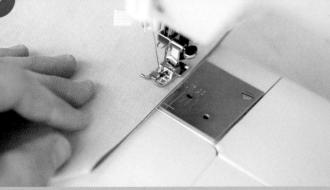

10 Spray **FoamFast 74 adhesive** onto bottom surface of **4" high density foam** that has been cut to size noted on blueprint.

11 Place foam onto plywood base (h) being careful to align with edges.

12 For extra comfort and loft, wrap a layer of **1" batting** around cushion and base, securing with spray adhesive. Pull batting over plywood firmly and staple all the way around, approximately 1" in from edge.

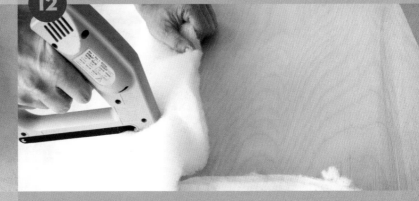

13 Trim off excess batting, making sure to remove bulk at corners.

14 Slide vinyl cushion cover over seat base and secure with a **staple gun.** For even tension, work back and forth on opposing sides while stapling.

15 Continue stapling all the way around. Flatten staples with a hammer to ensure that they are pressed all the way into the wood.

16 With cushion face down place bench base on top of cushion base (h) and carefully align. Using **1 $\frac{1}{4}$" screws,** attach the two parts together. Be sure that the

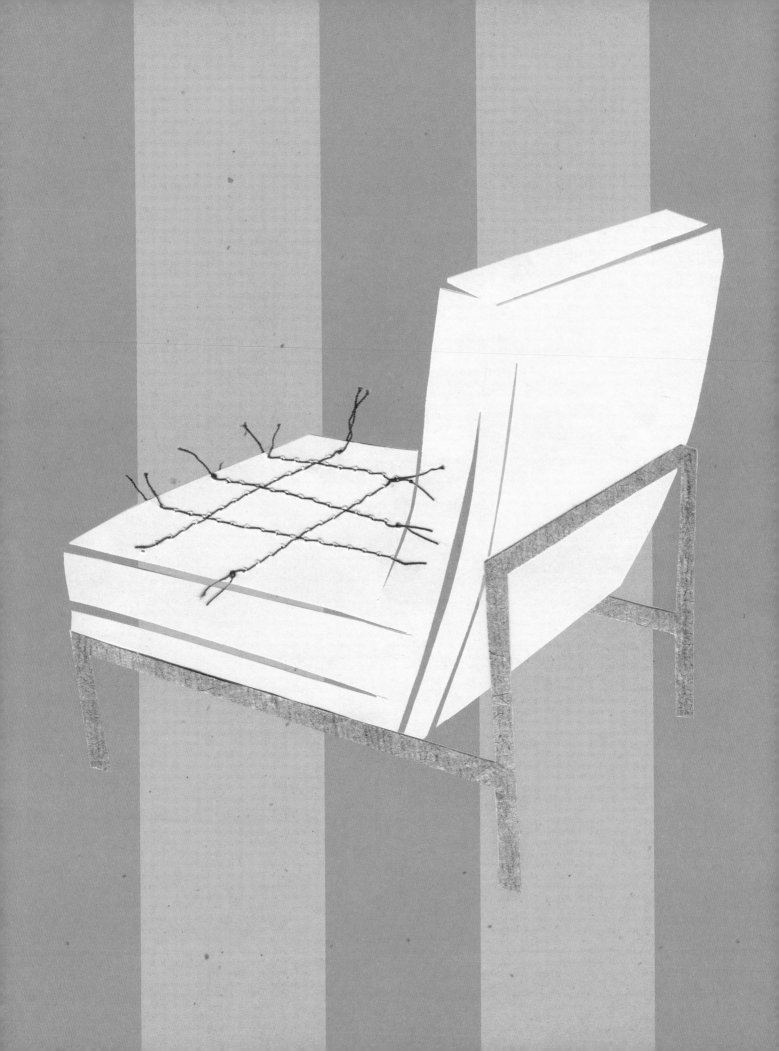

KNOLL

Today we take it for granted that designers are creative talents worthy of support and admiration. But in 1938, design and the people who do it for a living didn't quite have the universal cachet they enjoy now. Fortunately, that's the year a company called Knoll was founded. Headquartered in East Greenville, Pennsylvania, Knoll quickly became a legend, and deservedly so: the company was ahead of its time in putting design on a par with other creative art forms and producing furniture and accessories with astonishing staying power.

Knoll's corporate slogan is "Good design is good business"—a phrase coined by Florence Knoll, the designer who married Hans Knoll and encouraged him to champion her fellow designers. Among them were such giants as Ludwig Mies van der Rohe (Florence's onetime teacher), Marcel Breuer, Isamu Noguchi, Eero Saarinen, Harry Bertoia, Richard Schultz, Warren Platner, Hans Wegner, George Nakashima, Pierre Jeanneret (Le Corbusier's cousin), and Ralph Rapson. These visionaries created show-stopping work for Knoll that would become enduring modern classics and cult status items.

There are many more whose names perhaps have not become household words, but they too deserve equal credit as building blocks of Knoll's illustrious history. They include Jorgen Rasmussen, Don Petitt, Kurt Nordstrom, Don Albinson, Clay Michie, Donald R. Knorr, Lewis Butler, and the textile masterminds Eszter Haraszty and Anni Albers.

Proud of its legacy, the company exhibits over 150 examples of pivotal designs at the Knoll Museum in East Greenville, which is open by appointment. But most importantly, Knoll continues its commitment to creativity, manufacturing designs by a wide range of today's leading architects and designers, from Gae Aulenti to Frank Gehry to Maya Lin.

In a recent creative coup, the company hired the late Stephen Sprouse to design a collection of hand-lettered textiles. One of Sprouse's designs features a repeat of the phrase "Less is More"—a philosophy famously expressed by Mies van der Rohe and before him, by the poet Robert Browning in 1855. In a wittily self-referential flourish, Knoll displayed Sprouse's artfully scribbled fabric in its showroom by using it to upholster one of the most recognized chairs in the world: the Barcelona by Mies van der Rohe (which Knoll has continuously manufactured since 1948).

As famous as that chair has become, there's one that's perhaps even more widely known, and Knoll had a hand in that too: the ingenious folding marvel known as the Butterfly, first designed by Pierre Hardoy in 1938. After the company acquired the United States production rights to the Butterfly in 1947, the market became flooded with copies—but after a protracted legal battle, Knoll lost its claim of copyright infringement in 1951. More than five million copies are estimated to have been produced during the 1950s alone, and today the Butterfly remains one of the most enduringly popular items of stylish, popularly priced furniture. Which, in an ironically roundabout way, merely proves the timeless truth of Knoll's slogan: Good design really is good business.

RING-STITCHED LAP BLANKET

Nothing's more comforting than a hand-sewn quilt. This one has a mod motif thanks to the wide-stitched circles—and an elegant look thanks to the union of two fine fabrics, velveteen on one side and satin on the other.

EASE
LEVEL
2

1 Cut out one piece of **shiny satin** and one piece of **velveteen**, 48" x 40" each. Cut out a piece of **thin batting** to the same size.

With satin and velveteen right sides together and batting on top, sew all the way around using a ¹/₂" seam allowance. Leave a 6" opening on one side to turn it right side out. **2**

3 Clip all four corners to remove excess bulk.

Turn right side out and press seams flat. Close opening by handstitching. **4**

5 Using a **quilter's pen with disappearing ink,** trace nine 9" circles (we used a **bucket** as a guide) onto the velveteen side, spacing them equally in three stripes of three.

Choose four or five colors of **variegated embroidery floss.** Quilt around the circles with ¹/₂" stitches, alternating thread color with each circle. Finally, stitch around the diameter of the entire blanket, about ¹/₂" from the sides. **6**

ILLUMINATED WOOD TILE HEADBOARD

EASE
LEVEL
4

At 7 feet high, this headboard makes a dramatic statement. But its monumental proportions are softened by the grid of plywood squares, each tinted a warm honey color that's so golden and soothing. A recessed light channel mounted behind the headboard washes onto the wall from behind, throwing the most flattering possible amber glow on the walls—and your skin.

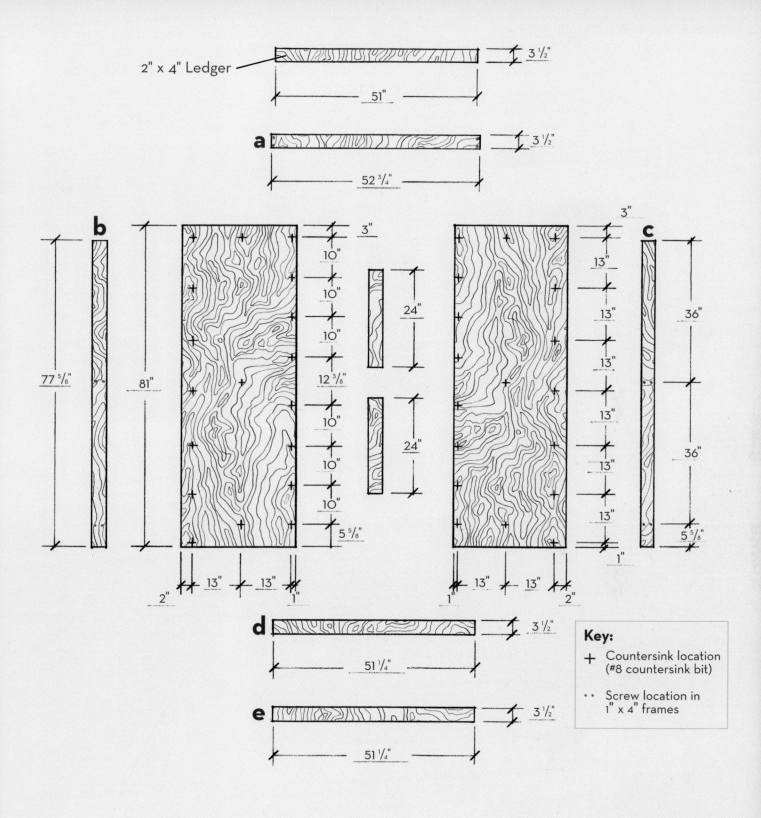

2" x 4" Ledger

3 1/2"

51"

a 3 1/2"

52 3/4"

b

77 5/8"

81"

3"

10"

10"

10"

12 3/8"

10"

10"

10"

5 5/8"

24"

24"

3"

13"

13"

13"

13"

13"

13"

36"

36"

5 5/8"

1"

c

2" 13" 13" 1"

1" 13" 13" 2"

d 3 1/2"

51 1/4"

e 3 1/2"

51 1/4"

Key:

+ Countersink location
   (#8 countersink bit)

·· Screw location in
    1" x 4" frames

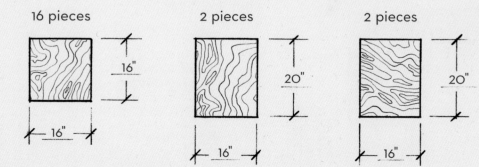

16 pieces

16"

16"

2 pieces

20"

16"

2 pieces

20"

16"

1 Have all wood cut, and predrill according to blueprint. Remove rough edges with **120 grit sandpaper.** Prestain 15" x 15" wood tile pieces. Using **1 5/8" drywall screws,** attach top (a) to sides (b and c). Then attach center support (d) and bottom support (e).

2 To prepare headboard face, lay one piece of **3/8" AC plywood** face up on the floor and attach two **1" x 4" cleats** through face using **1" screws.** Make sure that screw heads are recessed below surface.

3 Lay second piece of 3/8" AC plywood on floor face up, align with other piece and attach to cleats using 1" screws.

4 Lean assembled pieces of plywood against wall and mark outline of 1" x 4" frame. Place 1" x 4" frame on floor and lay plywood pieces face up on frame.

5 After making bottom edge of 3/8" plywood flush with frame and aligning with outline marks, attach plywood to frame using **1 1/4" drywall screws.** It is very important that screw heads are below surface of plywood.

6 With assembled headboard lying face up, brush and wipe off entire surface to make sure it is clean. Starting along center seam, brush **glue** on using a **2 1/2" brush.** It is a good idea to mix the glue with a little water to keep glue from drying too fast. Add 1/4 cup of water for every two cups of glue.

TIP

A ledger is a wall-mounted support brace that allows a construction to rest on top of it and provides a secure and hidden attachment to the wall

7 Apply panels so that the directions of the wood grain alternate. Make sure that center seam is consistent and that enough glue is applied. When all panels have been set in place, check for any raised or uneven edges. Let dry overnight.

8 Once assembly has dried, stand it up vertically, leaning the face against a wall. Stain the visible sides of the 1" x 4" frame. Once stain has dried to the touch, use a **staple gun** and attach **white zip ties** where 1" x 4" frame meets back of plywood. Place zip ties approximately every 18".

9 Place **light rope** into open zip ties such that the location of the power source is considered. Once the layout looks good, tighten the zip ties around the light rope.

10 Next, attach the ledger to the wall at 78" from finished floor using a **level.** We suggest attaching the first piece directly into studs and then attaching the second piece to the first. Be sure to carefully align the second piece.

11 Lift assembled headboard onto ledger. Press firmly against wall. Have a friend hold the piece if necessary while you get ready to attach it. If you have notched the frame for the baseboard, check the fit.

12 Drilling through top piece of frame, attach headboard to ledger. Use at least **three 1½" wood screws** (right corner, left corner, and center). You may also want to attach the headboard at its base. To do this, just use a **small angle bracket** on both sides either into the baseboard or floor.

TIP

A cleat is a wooden support that crosses over the seam between two pieces of wood that are joined together without overlapping.

FLOATING BED PLATFORM

Perched on out-of-sight recessed legs, this slab of ³/₄" plywood with lattice trim, left mostly au naturel and stained around the edges, gives the appearance of floating in space—a magic trick I love. Plus, it allows for easy vacuuming under the bed!

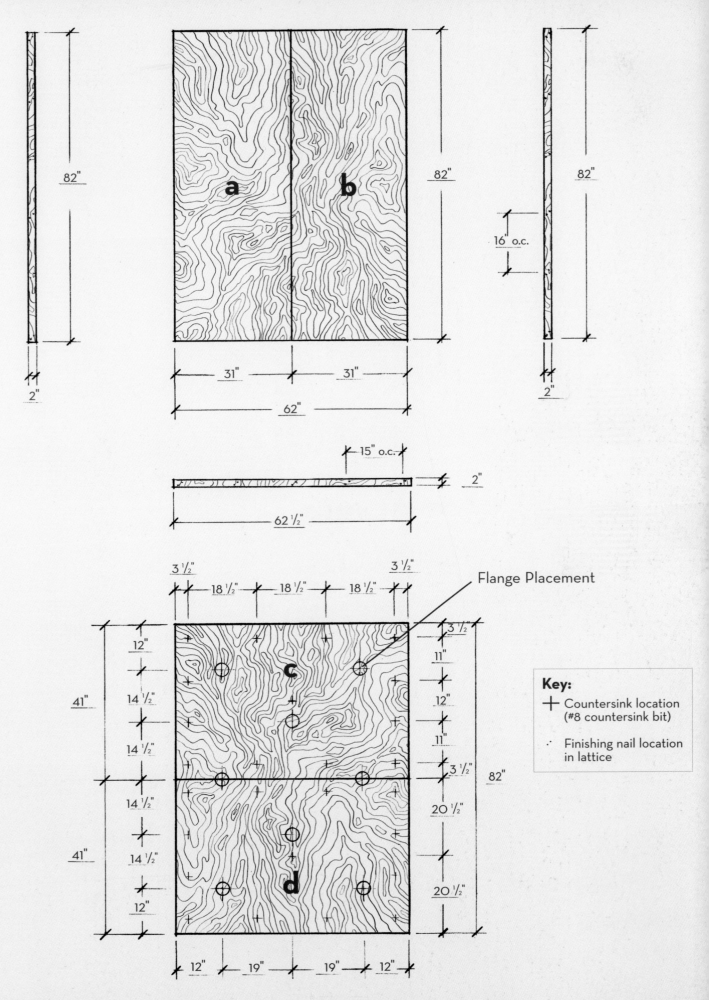

82"

2"

a   b

82"

31"   31"

62"

82"

16" o.c.

2"

15" o.c.

2"

62 ½"

3 ½"   3 ½"

18 ½"   18 ½"   18 ½"

Flange Placement

12"

3 ½

11"

41"

14 ½"

c

12"

14 ½"

11"

3 ½"

14 ½"

82"

20 ½"

41"

14 ½"

d

20 ½"

12"

Key:
+ Countersink location
(#8 countersink bit)
∴ Finishing nail location
in lattice

12"   19"   19"   12"

1

Have all wood cut, and predrill according to blueprint. Remove rough edges with **120 grit sandpaper** and wipe down with a **tack cloth.** Lay long pieces (a) and (b) of ³/₄" plywood face down. Arrange pieces so the factory cut edges are facing each other down the center.

2

Lay wide piece (c) on top of long pieces and align outside edges. Attach pieces together using ³/₄" **drywall screws,** making sure to sink screws just below surface of wood.

3

Lay second wide piece (d) on long pieces and align with edges. Attach with ³/₄" drywall screws.

4

Place **pipe flanges** as shown on blueprint and attach.

5 Clean ³/₄" **diameter pipe legs** with **mineral spirits** and thread pipes into flanges, turning until they are tight. Place 1 ¹/₈" **diameter rubber caps** on ends of legs. Turn upright and set into place.

Sand edges of platform using **150 grit sandpaper,** making sure not to round edges. Brush off dust thoroughly. Apply **wood glue** to back of **lattice** pieces.

6

7 Attach lattice using **finishing nails,** starting with side pieces. You might need a helping hand with this step, as long pieces are unruly. Allow glue to dry completely.

Since your mattress will cover most of the platform, you need only stain the outside edge, up to 8" in from both sides and the end. Apply **stain** to both the plywood and lattice. Allow to dry and finish with two coats **water based polyurethane.**

8

JULIUS
SHULMAN

The Case Study Houses
were conceived as accessible housing—yet today, they are regarded as very fancy affairs, priceless specimens of American architecture. But appreciating those experimental structures for the treasures they are would not have been possible without the photographs of Julius Shulman.

As an architectural photographer, Shulman's aim was to "present an architect's design effort to the world." He did that beautifully, making Case Study Houses look glamorous and expensive, even though they were made of the simplest components. His camera accorded these structures—and, indeed, every structure he photographed, from factory exteriors to office-building lobbies—the same respect he gave to the most exalted buildings by Frank Lloyd Wright.

The way Shulman framed his shots is so artful. There's nothing extraneous in his images. He managed to offer lots of visual information simultaneously, and he could really crop where needed. I keep thinking of his photograph of Pierre Koenig's Case Study House #21 (1958), with a woman in a robin's-egg-blue dress seated on a sofa, and a man in a gray flannel suit standing beside a wood-and-metal credenza. That image shows that the Case Study Houses were as livable as they were stylish.

Much more than chronicling the way buildings looked, Shulman conveyed what it was like to be inside them. From the way he manipulated light, the viewer can almost feel the texture of the stones comprising a wall, or the planks of a poolside deck. Shulman was the custodian of images, of course, but more than that, he was the custodian of an intangible, sublime feeling. His eyes have it.

SWEET DREAMS SHEET SET

A bedroom shouldn't be soft and soothing all the time. Create some excitement by making up plain white sheets with circular block prints in mustard, orange, and berry—deeper, hotter hues from the same color family as the pale ambers and corals in the rest of the suite. It's easy to do: simply dip the rim of a paper cup in different colors of fabric dye, and have fun imprinting rings on your sheets and pillowcases!

EASE
2
LEVEL

1 Before you begin, wash and iron all bedding. To prepare **pillowcases** for printing, insert a piece of **cardboard,** so paint doesn't soak through.

2 Line up **plastic cups** along the outside edge for pattern placement. Pour a $\frac{1}{8}$" deep puddle of **fabric paint** (magenta, orange, and mustard) onto **plastic plates.**

3 Gently dip one end of a cup into mustard colored paint and stamp onto pillowcase, gently twisting as you pull the cup off, so paint doesn't splatter. Remove place holder cups as you go.

4 Make a matching dot stripe in orange, above the mustard dot stripe. After the first two have dried, stamp a magenta dot stripe centered on top of the first two stripes.

5 For the **flat sheet,** stamp a dot stripe in alternating colors 4" down along the top edge.

6 For the **duvet cover,** use **large cups** and stamp all the way around the outside edge of the duvet cover in magenta. Use the smaller, bottom rim of the cup to stamp a smaller concentric circle in the center of the big circles, using orange paint.

7 For next concentric rectangle, repeat printing process using mustard paint on the outside ring and magenta paint on the inside ring.

8 For next concentric rectangle, repeat printing process using orange paint on the outside ring and mustard paint on the inside ring.

9 For final concentric rectangle, repeat printing process using magenta paint on the outside ring and orange paint on the inside ring.

10 To ensure the color fastness of the paint, heat-set with an **iron** on the backside of the fabric after paint has dried thoroughly.

HAND - QUILTED

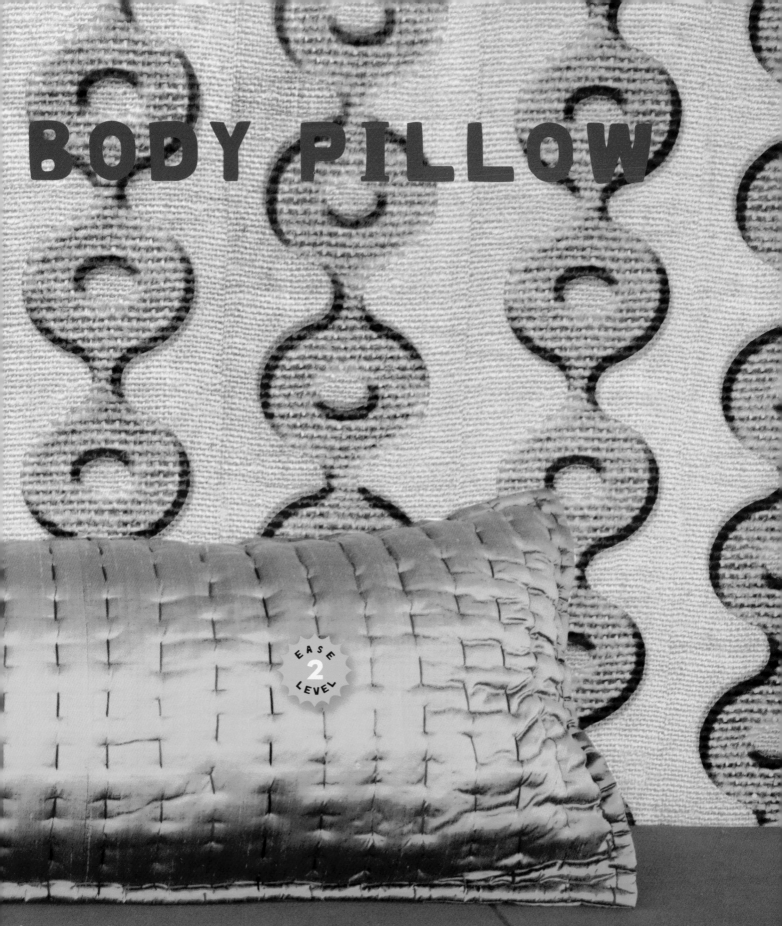

BODY PILLOW

EASE LEVEL 2

When you saddle-stitch sumptuous silk shantung with a large embroidery needle, the result is a Handmade Modern effect that's at once rough-hewn and elegant—and a lovely twenty-first-century update on old-fashioned handmade quilts.

1 Cut three pieces of **raw silk** at 55" x 22 ½" (front piece), 47 ½" x 22 1 ½" (back piece 1) and 18" x 22 ½" (back piece 2). Cut a piece of **1" thick batting** the same size as the front piece, 55" x 22 ½".

Edge stitch the front piece to batting around all four sides using a ¼" seam allowance. **2**

3 To create the quilting stitch pattern, use a **quilter's pen** to mark the front piece with stitch lines that are dotted at 1" intervals. Each stripe should be 2" apart, and continue across the entire length of the pillow.

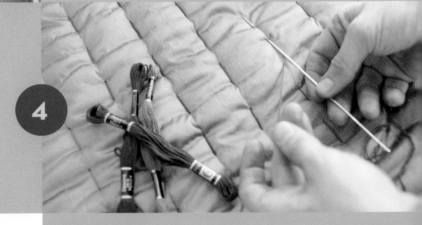

Thread an **8" upholstery needle** with a double length of **cotton embroidery floss,** and stitch through at dot marks to create 1" long stitches. Alternate colors to create a varied stripe. **4**

5 To create the "envelope" style back, hem one 22 ½" end of each back piece with a 1" finished roll hem.

6 Pin both back pieces onto front piece with right sides together, matching edges and letting back pieces overlap. Stitch all the way around, using a ½" seam allowance.

7 For a crisp corner, trim off excess fabric and batting, ¼" away from the stitch line to remove bulk.

8 To create a finished border, turn pillowcase right side out and mark a line for stitching at 1" intervals around the entire border, 1" in from the edge.

9 Using the 8" upholstery needle and one color of embroidery floss, stitch a line of 1" stitches all the way around the border.

10 Stuff with a **body pillow** through the envelope opening in the back.

BEDSIDE LIBRARY

EASE
3
LEVEL

This nightstand-taboret is stained honey to coordinate with the headboard; its prefab conical legs come from the hardware store. This piece is great for magazine and book storage, and it's especially convenient for a nighttime pitcher of water. There's no need to worry about annoying water rings on wood surfaces, because the berry-tinted cork top doubles as a giant, decorative coaster for middle-of-the-night drinks. The nice, soft texture of cork is very pleasant to the touch, and helps absorb sound, another plus in a quiet boudoir.

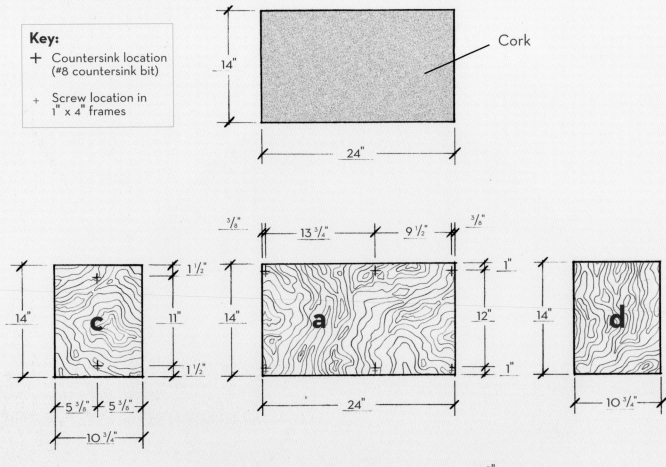

Cork

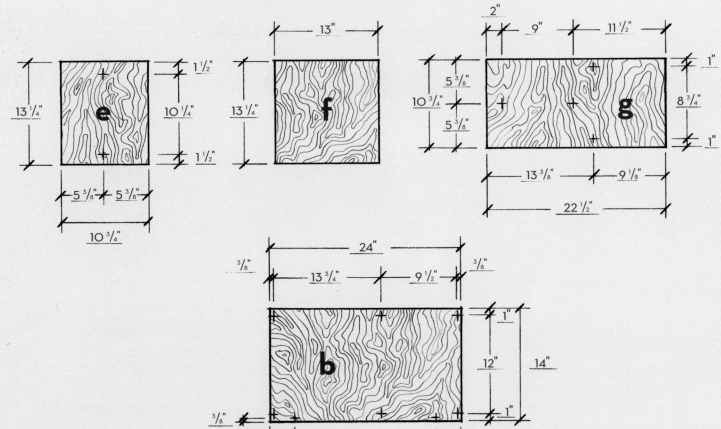

1

ave all wood cut, and predrill according to blueprint. To further prepare wood, follow steps 1–4 of Beauty Station (page 84).

2

Mark location for horizontal shelf (f) on vertical support (e) and predrill for finishing nails.

3

For added strength, apply a thin bead of **wood glue** to outside edge of shelf piece (f).

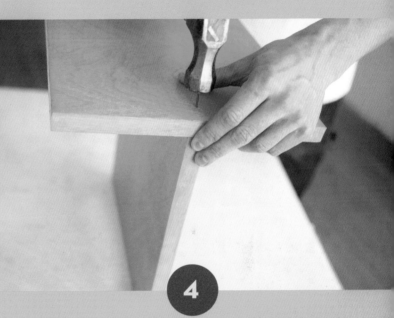

4

Attach interior pieces (e) and (f) to each other using **finishing nails.**

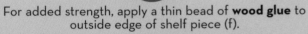

5

Mark locations for interior pieces and attach through back piece (g) using **1 3/8" drywall screws.**

6

Line up outside edges of base (b) with back and attach through center support using drywall screws.

7 Attach base (b) to interior vertical support piece (e) using **1 5/8" drywall screws.**

8 Attach side pieces (c) and (d) through base using drywall screws.

9 To secure horizontal shelf (f) to side piece (c) hammer together using **1 1/2" finishing nails.**

10 Attach side piece (d) through base (b) using drywall screws.

11 After applying a thin bead of **wood glue** to all exposed top edges, carefully set top piece (a) on assembly.

Attach top (a) using finishing nails, being careful not to dent surface. **12**

13 Stain and seal a 16" x 26" piece of ¼" **thick cork** using watered-down **fabric dye** and **polyurethane.** Attach to tabletop using wood glue. For a secure bond, allow glue to dry with table turned upside down on a plastic drop cloth.

Attach **angled leg brackets** ³/₄" in from sides on all four corners as shown. **14**

15 Leaving the unit face down, thread legs into brackets and tighten until secure.

With unit upside down on a cutting surface, trim off excess cork using an **X-Acto blade.**

The beauty of crafting with ribbons is the endless variety of possible patterns: By altering the width and color of the ribbons, you can create a simple checkerboard, a sophisticated grid— or your very own tartan, whether your clan has one or not!

EASE
LEVEL
2

WOVEN RIBBON PILLOWS

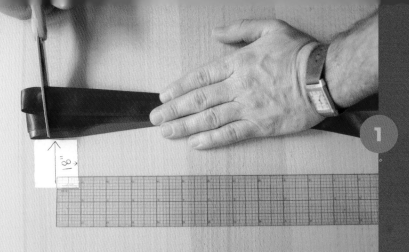

1 For a 16" x 16" pillow, you'll need a total of 38 pieces of $^7/_8$" **satin ribbon** in assorted colors. Cut each ribbon piece to 18" long.

2 Cut an 18" x 18" piece of **woven fusible interfacing** and place, fusible side up, on a piece of **foam core**. Begin laying ribbons in the color order you want.

3 Pin ribbons to interfacing in a straight row, creating your warp.

4 For the weft, start at the top, weaving in and out between the warp ribbons. Alternate the weaving pattern with every row. Pin each ribbon into place on both ends.

5 Once all your ribbons are woven together, lightly fuse ribbon to interfacing with a warm, dry iron. Remove all the pins and transfer entire piece to an ironing board to continue fusing, pressing on the backside of the interfacing.

6 Attach **decorative rope piping** to pillow face, by stitching around all sides and overlapping raw ends.

7 For the back, cut a 17" x 17" piece of **coordinating fabric** and sew with right sides together, leaving a 5" opening for turning and stuffing.

8 Turn pillow right side out, stuff with **Poly-Fil or a pillow blank,** and sew closed by hand.

COLOR
COPY
WALLPAPER

EASE
LEVEL
2

Existing wallpaper patterns can be so confining. It's more fun to get creative with graphic designs on the computer, color copy them at your local copy shop, then apply them directly to the wall with polyurethane for glamorous custom wall covering.

Create a design that will match up on all sides and create a repeated pattern. Measure your walls to determine the number of **color copies** you will need to have made. To avoid air bubbles, soak each sheet in water for a few seconds before applying.

1

2

To attach the color copies, apply a layer of **polyurethane** to the wall, using a pad brush. Place color copies on wall, matching pattern and overlapping ½" on all sides, and seal with a top coat of polyurethane.

Work from top to bottom and left to right, making sure to apply polyurethane in small sections to prevent it from drying before sheets are attached.

3

4

For a clean finished edge on corners, fold over your ½" overlap and seal well with polyurethane.

125

When designs resemble or suggest the forms of living organisms, whether intentionally or not, they're called biomorphic. And one of the founding mothers of biomorphic design is undoubtedly Eva Zeisel. Whether made of ceramic, wood, plastic, or steel, her ergonomically-considered creations don't just resemble living forms; they are infused with a vital energy all their own.

Objects designed by Zeisel possess a life force, and that force is so strong that these technically "inanimate" things appear ready to get up and dance around the room like living, breathing beings, recalling the expressive figures from the Disney movie *Fantasia*. Looking at Zeisel's work is like watching a shadow play of cartoon characters: it's sophisticated and fun at the same time. In Zeisel's world, porcelain salt-and-pepper shakers appear to be bending at the neck in a conspiratorial whisper, three tiny holes on one "head" suggesting two eyes and a mouth.

"All my work is mother-and-child," Zeisel has said. That sums up her achievement perfectly: like pregnant women, designs by Eva Zeisel glow from within as they appear to grow and change before our eyes. Observing them is like catching something wonderfully alive just as it's in the middle of shape-shifting. The brilliant Belly Button wall divider, on display in Los Angeles' Hollywood Standard Hotel, is a fine example: it's an iconically feminine network of voluptuous hourglass figures, each one punctuated with a navel-like indentation at its center.

"The designer has to have real contact with the audience, not just think about his or her self-expression," she once said. That strikes me as an admirably selfless philosophy for someone with such a consistently distinct style. Throughout Zeisel's long career, the integrity of her vision has been clearly evident, from her earliest work in the 1920s to the exciting designs she's creating for Nambe today. Everything she touches is futuristic and naturalistic at once—a combination I happen to love.

EVA ZEISEL

HANGING LANTERN TRIO

EASE
LEVEL
3

I was inspired by George Nelson's cluster lamps to design a Handmade Modern lighting solution just for the bedroom. Echoing the pattern on the Color Copy Wallpaper (page 124), these ethereal, sculptural shapes are each made of two ordinary lampshades découpaged with handmade rice paper in a sunburst pattern, then attached end-to-end. The glow from these lanterns is really spectacular, and so flattering to the complexion, because they're basically warm, makeup colors.

1. To cut lengths of **rice paper** strips, measure a conical lampshade, adding 1" for overlap. Fold the rice paper roadmap style and cut into strips, 2" wide by appropriate length.

2. In order to keep pattern straight, divide shade into four equal parts and apply strips using **Mod Podge** at quadrants.

3. Fill in quadrants, overlapping strips ⅛" on bottom as shown. Work toward the center of each quadrant.

4. For a clean finish, turn under top and bottom edges of each strip and secure.

5. Remove wire frame from bottom shade and repeat steps 1–4, using a contrasting colored paper. Attach shades together using a small bead of **Liquid Nails.**

6. To obscure the seam, apply a layer of Mod Podge across intersection.

7. Cut a length of appropriately colored **seam binding** and center over intersection, overlapping ends ½".

8. Carefully attach the **wires** to the **porcelain socket base,** making sure wires don't touch.

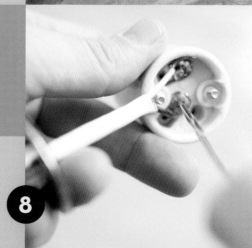

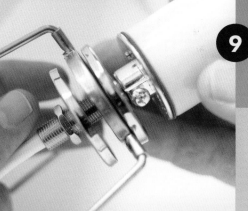

9 Attach **base, all-thread, washers and nuts** as shown, and tighten. Repeat steps 1–9 to make the two additional lamps.

10 To make a **paper** pattern for your wooden ceiling mount, cut a round-edged equilateral triangle that measures 17" on each side.

11 To determine placement of drill holes, draw a second triangle, 1 ½" smaller than the cut edge of the first, puncturing pattern at triangle points.

12 Trace pattern onto a piece of ½" **plywood,** and carefully cut out with a **jigsaw.**

13 Drill all three holes using a ½" **drill bit.** To avoid splintering, apply **tape** to wood prior to drilling. Sand and stain triangular wood piece.

14 Using ½" plywood, create a junction box with **two pieces of 3" x 6" wood,** and **two pieces of 3" x 5" wood.** Drill a ½" hole centered into both of the 3" x 6" pieces, and one hole into each of the 3" x 5" pieces, centered and 1 ½" in from edge.

15 Attach a 1 ¼" **L-bracket** to one 3" x 6" piece as shown. Repeat on other 3" x 6" at opposite end.

16 Assemble your square junction box with **finishing nails,** placing the 3" x 6" pieces on top of the 3" x 5" pieces, as shown.

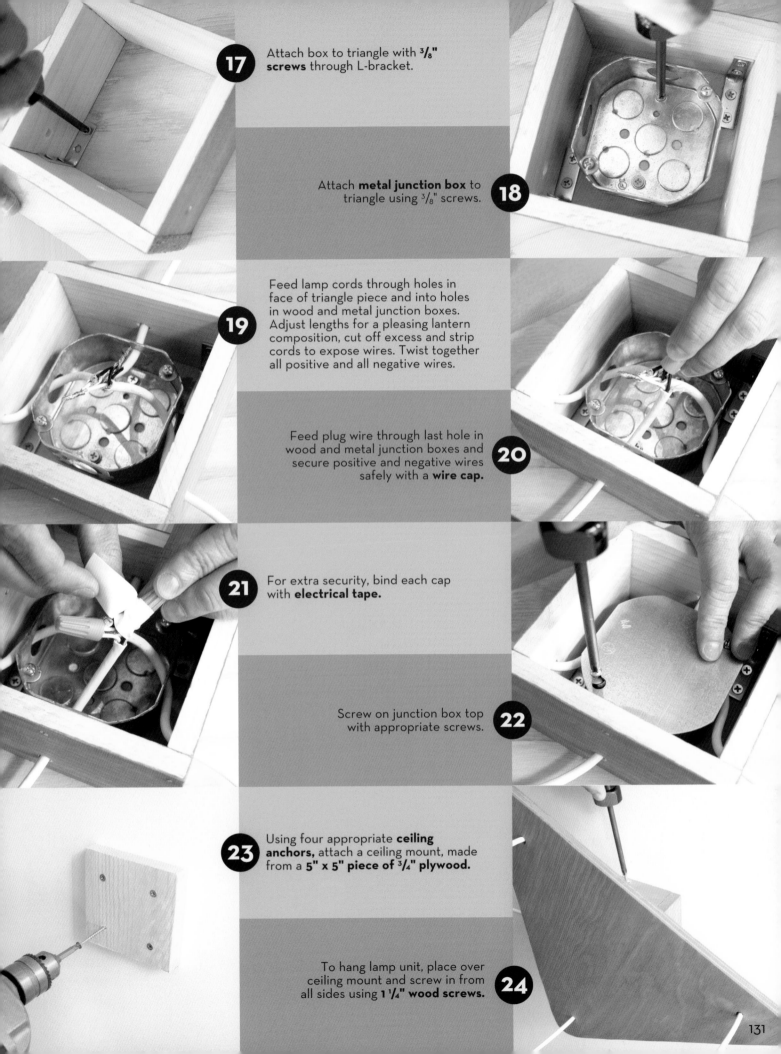

17 Attach box to triangle with ⅜" **screws** through L-bracket.

18 Attach **metal junction box** to triangle using ⅜" screws.

19 Feed lamp cords through holes in face of triangle piece and into holes in wood and metal junction boxes. Adjust lengths for a pleasing lantern composition, cut off excess and strip cords to expose wires. Twist together all positive and all negative wires.

20 Feed plug wire through last hole in wood and metal junction boxes and secure positive and negative wires safely with a **wire cap.**

21 For extra security, bind each cap with **electrical tape.**

22 Screw on junction box top with appropriate screws.

23 Using four appropriate **ceiling anchors,** attach a ceiling mount, made from a **5" x 5" piece of ¾" plywood.**

24 To hang lamp unit, place over ceiling mount and screw in from all sides using 1¼" **wood screws.**

NAKED DRESSER DRESS-UP

EASE LEVEL 2

Unpainted, untreated wood furniture is a great surface for the application of personal style. But painting or staining the wood aren't the only ways to go. Here, handmade Japanese rice paper is applied with varnish and a paintbrush like wallpaper, for a lovely decorative overlay that doesn't completely obscure the beauty of the wood grain beneath.

1 Stain an **unfinished dresser,** leaving the drawer fronts unfinished. Trace around the face of each drawer onto **colored rice paper,** leaving a 1" overlap for wrapping around all the edges.

2 Paint a thin coat of **water-based polyurethane** onto the drawers and apply the paper.

3 Paint another coat of polyurethane on top to seal.

4 Using your **paintbrush,** seal all edges on the back side with polyurethane.

5 Trim off excess paper with an **X-Acto blade.**

6 Paint **round wooden drawer pulls** with **glitter nailpolish** and attach.

UTENSIL TRAY
MAKEOVER

Why not repurpose silverware trays to hold and organize makeup, jewelry, or hair ornaments? Simply choose a wood tray to coordinate with the Beauty Station, and tuck it right into the opening—or anywhere you have a little unused space. Lining the tray compartments in colorful felt makes the contents easier to differentiate, and gives the effect of a Mondrian pattern.

EASE LEVEL 1

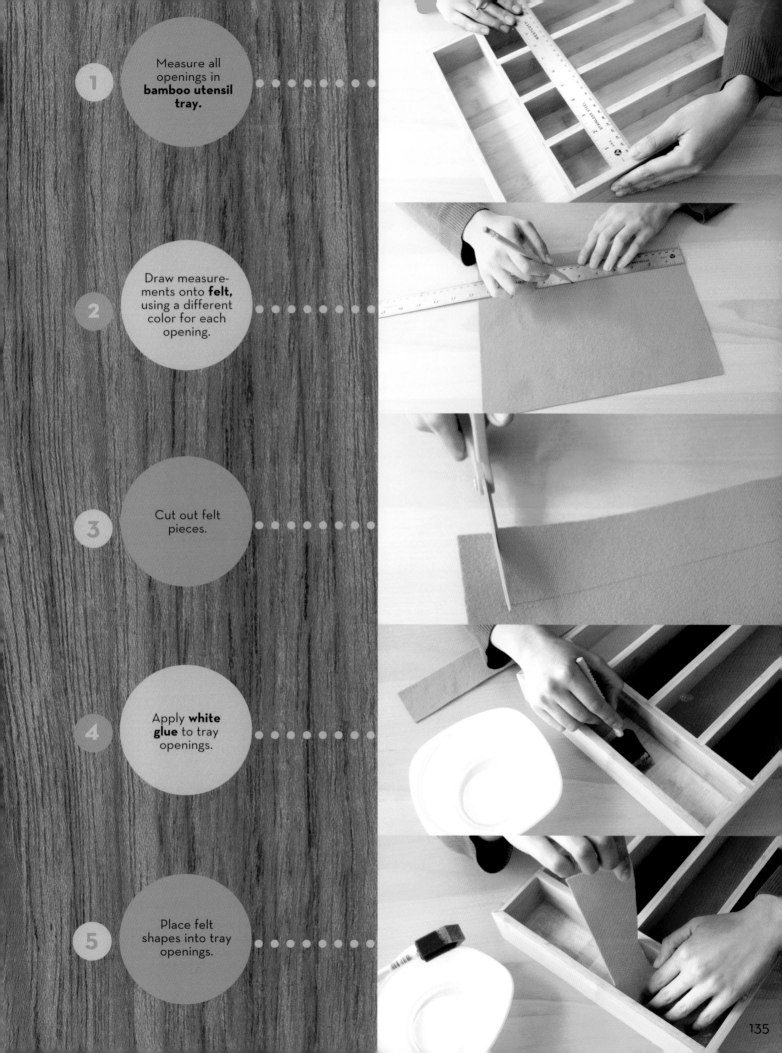

1 Measure all openings in **bamboo utensil tray.**

2 Draw measurements onto **felt,** using a different color for each opening.

3 Cut out felt pieces.

4 Apply **white glue** to tray openings.

5 Place felt shapes into tray openings.

BRIGHT IDEA
LAMP SAVER

Rehabilitate an unsightly old lamp (or a nondescript new one) by concentrically gluing space-dyed cotton rope all the way around it, from top to bottom. For a topper worthy of such a lovely base, cover a paper shade with straw paper from your local art-supply store. The shade filters the light softly, creating precisely the flattering effect you want at your beauty station.

EASE
2
LEVEL

1

Wind 20 yards ⅜" **cotton rope** into a [sk]ein that is 1 yard long and loosely tie off at four equally spaced sections.

2

Prepare four colors of **fabric dye** in separate **buckets**. Dip two ends of the rope skein into two dye baths for 10 minutes.

3

Repeat process with two remaining dye baths. Rinse entire length of rope in warm water until it runs clear. Let dry.

4

[U]sing a **hot glue gun**, begin wrapping your [l]amp base with the space-dyed rope, starting at the top and working down.

5

Continue wrapping, applying glue in small sections as you go.

6

When you reach the bottom, coil the rope into a spiral and trim off excess.

7

[M]ake a lampshade pattern onto **textured** [p]aper by tracing the top and bottom of the shade as you roll it across the paper.

8

Coat lampshade and back side of pattern with **spray adhesive**. Stuff paper into lampshade to avoid spraying glue on interior.

9

Carefully apply textured paper pattern to cover lampshade, overlapping edge.

BURLAP BEAUTY BOOST

Gold picture frames can look too formal in a bedroom, where every detail should exude intimacy and warmth. Cover the frame with the computer-generated burlap pattern that's the background of the Color Copy Wallpaper. Put a mirror in the frame for a rare, wonderfully multi-dimensional effect—the frame actually matches the wallpaper!

EASE
2
LEVEL

1

Remove glass and backing from mirror frame and set aside. Create a pattern for each side out of **heavy duty kraft paper,** mitering the corners.

2

Create artwork on the computer and print. Fold in half lengthwise so you can cut out two at a time.

3

If your pattern piece is larger than your paper, fold pattern piece in half and trace onto printed paper, adding a ½" allowance for overlap.

4

Apply **Mod Podge** to frame with a **foam pad brush.**

5

Apply printed paper, lining up the corner with the mitered edge.

6

Add an overcoat of Mod Podge and trim corners. Reattach mirror and backing.

SCALLOPED EDGE AREA RUG

EASE
LEVEL
2

A carpet knife can turn ordinary carpet tiles into delightful, custom floor covering: artwork you can walk on. Using a template, simply carve carpet squares into scallop shapes, then cut teardrops for the corners. The best part: If something spills on one of the tiles, you don't have to clean the whole rug—the adhesive backing is low-tack, so simply lift up the stained tiles and replace them with new ones.

1

The interior of the rug is made up of full squares of **InterfaceFLOR "Solid Ground" carpet tiles in Red 882508.** To create the outside scallop detail, make a pattern onto **kraft paper** that is the same size as one square carpet tile. Fold into quadrants, and trace a circle onto it using a **pen** and a **piece of string.**

2

Calculate how many tiles you need to create the border. Unfold the paper pattern and cut out half the circle to create a scallop pattern. Trace onto the carpet tiles you've set aside for your border, and cut cautiously with a **utility knife.**

3

For the corner pieces, trace ¾ of a circle onto the carpet tile to make a teardrop shape.

4

Lay down square pieces of the area rug, peeling and sticking corner adhesives as you go.

5

Apply round edged border pieces to complete.

THRIFTY THRONE

When it was discovered in the trash, this chair was dark brown, its seat half torn off. After a thorough sanding, it was primed, then painted high-sheen gold with spray paint. Wrapping the back with space-dyed cotton rope yields a fuzzy striped pattern that coordinates nicely with the new peach-toned velveteen seat cushion. All in all, a Handmade Modern seat fit for regal digs!

EASE
2
LEVEL

1 Prepare your chair frame by removing upholstered parts, sanding down wooden frame with sandpaper, and securing any loose joints with glue.

2 To prepare the wood for painting, spray on at least one coat of **primer** in a well ventilated area.

3 After primer is dry, apply several light coats of **gold spray paint.**

4 To reinforce seat, staple a piece of **canvas** all the way around the edge with a **staple gun.**

5 For a more comfortable cushion, wrap seat with **batting** and staple on underside.

6 Wrap a piece of **velveteen** around seat and staple to underside.

7 Cut off excess fabric at corners and **hammer** down staples until flat.

8 For a tidy look, attach a layer of vinyl to the bottom of cushion and attach with staple gun.

9 Using the same ³/₈" **space-dyed cord** as on the Bright Idea Lamp Saver (page 136), wrap around the back piece of the chair, and attach with a **hot glue gun.**

10 Continue wrapping and hot gluing until back piece is completely covered. Secure the cut end by tucking it behind the wrapped cord, and glue.

143

And yet, incredibly, this treasure never achieved household-name status. The breadth of Rapson's achievement is phenomenal. He deserves to be mentioned in the same sentence as Girard, the Eameses, and George Nelson.

I love his fanciful approach to design; it's serious fun, Bauhaus-sharp but at the same time quite charming, cheerful, and even traditional. He's never been afraid of a decorative flourish. It's always brave and tricky to make pretty things in a world where that's not applauded, and there's a real bravery to Rapson's work. And his chairs, especially the Rapson Rapid Rocker, are so

RALPH RAPSON

Ralph Rapson was a contemporary of many of the biggest names in architecture and design, including Eero Saarinen and Florence Knoll, and contributed a dynamic design to the Case Study Program. Whether for buildings or furnishings, exteriors or interiors, Rapson's timeless designs hold their own alongside the mid-century big guns, and they're every bit as exciting as the work of today's edgiest young talents.

ergonomically considered, they invite you to sit in them longer. He really put comfort first.

His base for the past five decades has been Minneapolis; the city and its environs are home to many of his defining projects, including the Prince of Peace Lutheran Church for the Deaf, the Philip and Eleanor Pillsbury House, and the Tyrone Guthrie Theater. Sadly, the latter two buildings were torn down, despite public outcries

to save them. The Pillsbury House, especially, was a zenith in modern architecture. The spatial qualities on the ceiling alone were spectacular, and the perforated panels in the kitchen were just so sweet. It's outrageous that this masterpiece isn't there any more.

Rapson's sketches are a pleasure to behold. He has such a modern hand, and his drawings from decades ago look so contemporary. "I'm always designing or doodling something," Rapson says. "Drawing and design are the same thing for me." I would love to have Ralph Rapson build a house for me. In fact, he could just take scissors to one of his old designs and tape it back together, and I'm sure it'd be brilliant and wonderful.

At 89, the principal of Rapson Architects stands by his motto, "Keep designing." The master builder still goes to the office every day. "I don't want to retire," he says. "I expect to be carried off on my drafting board! For me, architecture is not work."

RELAXING READING ROOM

Ah, the three R's . . . but this time around, the 'rithmetic is easy and fun. It's as simple as adding all your Handmade Modern components together to create the ultimate mod library-cum-exhibition space, with shelves for artwork and collectibles as well as books. By the way, a library needn't be bland or neutral. I believe it can and should be a colorful, stimulating place that administers a brain massage even before you crack open a book. This is my favorite spot for sitting down to read an exciting new title—or revisit a cherished old one. As for that other R, even writing checks is a pleasure in an environment like this!

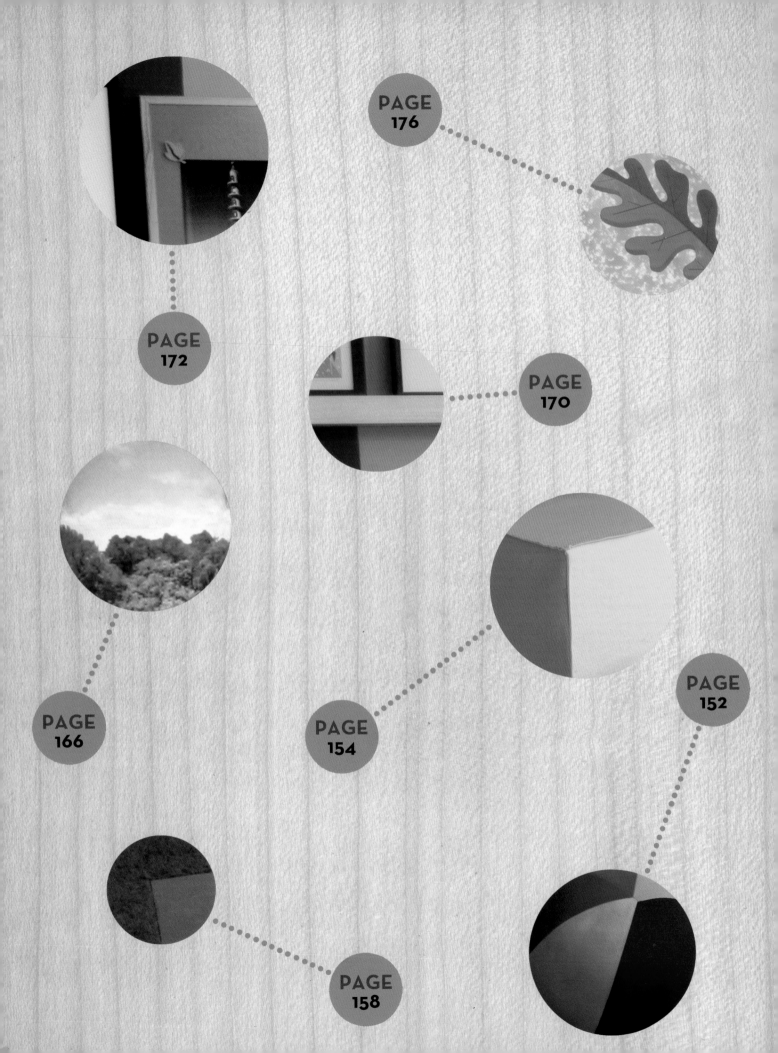

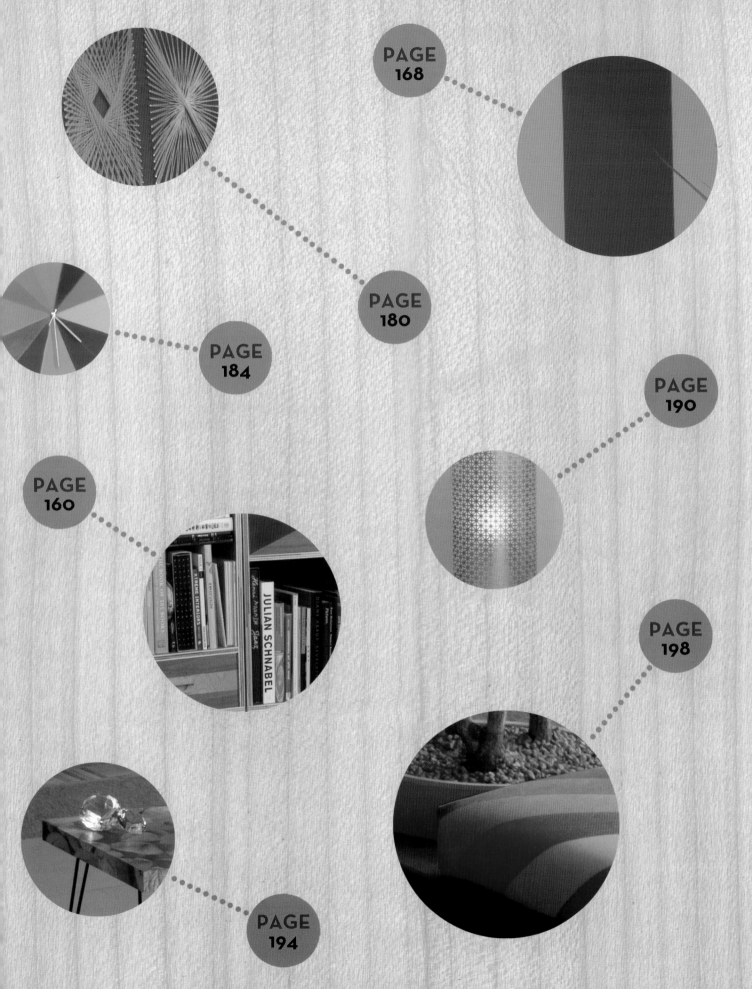

BEACH BALL PILLOW

EASE
LEVEL
2

These gumball-colored felt pillows are quite ergonomically correct, nestling right into the crook of your neck to double as a head rest. They provide just the levity called for to make a library quietly entertaining: it's impossible to be too serious or scholarly in their presence.

Pattern

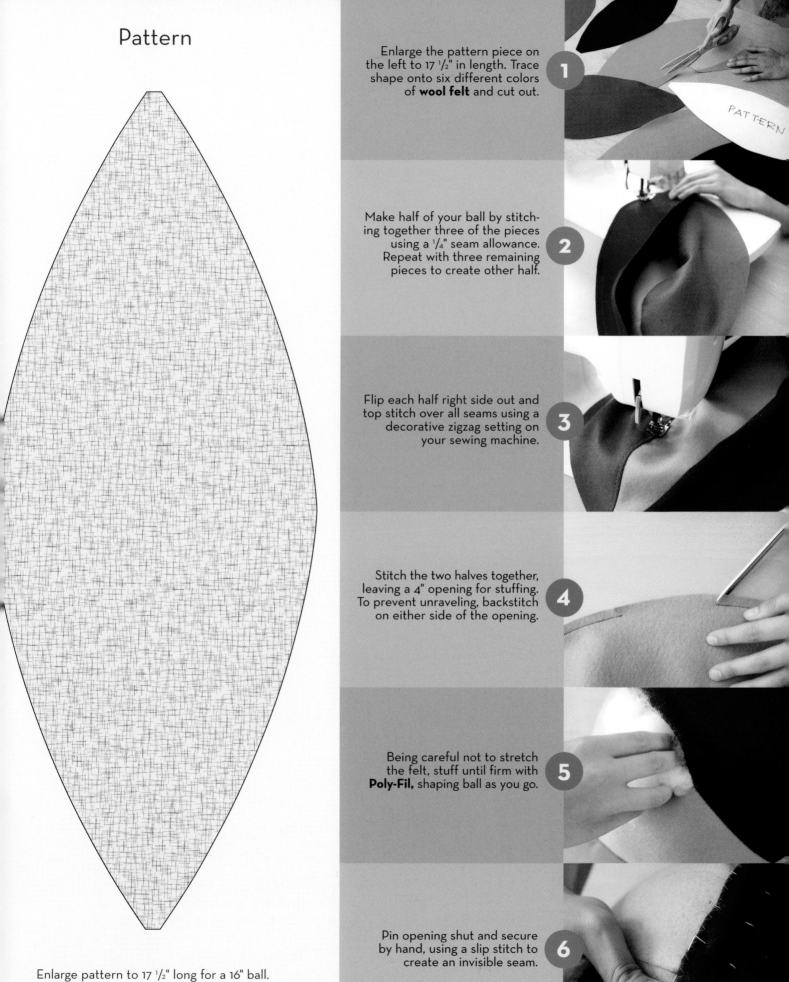

Enlarge pattern to 17 ½" long for a 16" ball.
Enlarge pattern to 15 ½" long for a 14" ball.
Enlarge pattern to 13 ½" long for a 12" ball.

1 Enlarge the pattern piece on the left to 17 ½" in length. Trace shape onto six different colors of **wool felt** and cut out.

2 Make half of your ball by stitching together three of the pieces using a ¼" seam allowance. Repeat with three remaining pieces to create other half.

3 Flip each half right side out and top stitch over all seams using a decorative zigzag setting on your sewing machine.

4 Stitch the two halves together, leaving a 4" opening for stuffing. To prevent unraveling, backstitch on either side of the opening.

5 Being careful not to stretch the felt, stuff until firm with **Poly-Fil,** shaping ball as you go.

6 Pin opening shut and secure by hand, using a slip stitch to create an invisible seam.

153

CHROMATIC CUBE

EASE
3
LEVEL

Employing a different happy shade of pink for each side, these fun-filled, foam-filled cubes are as easily tossed around as a pair of dice—and so soft, their edges can't cause injury to kids or pets.

1

Using six tonal colors of **wool felt,** cut out six pieces, each measuring 18 ½" square. Cut out three more pieces for closure facings, each measuring 3" x 18 ½", in the color you chose for the bottom of the cube.

2

Begin by sewing all side seams together. Lay two felt squares on top of each other and sew along one edge using a ½" seam allowance. Since all the seams on the cube are exposed on the outside, stop ½" from the top and bottom edges and backstitch to secure each seam. Repeat this step until you've sewn all four sides of the cube together.

3

Attach top to cube body by sewing around all four sides in the same manner as described in step 2.

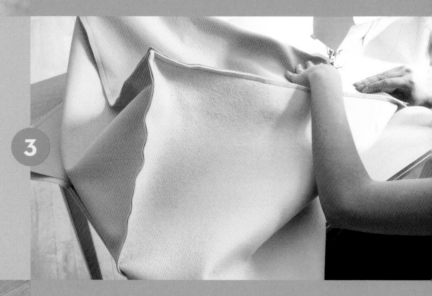

4

Miter the corners on your three rectangular facing pieces, by trimming at a 45-degree angle as shown. The pieces will line up at right angles to each other. Sew one side of **Velcro** 1 ½" in from outside edges, as shown.

5

Attach all three facing pieces to three sides of the body using a ¹/₂" seam allowance, stopping ¹/₂" from the top and bottom of edges and backstitching to secure each seam.

6

Sew opposing sides of all Velcro, using an edge stitch, along three sides of your bottom square of felt, 1 ¹/₂" in from outside edges.

7

Cut out a piece of **rubber shelf liner** that is 17" x 17" and attach to reverse side of bottom felt piece to give the cube a non-skid surface. To stop the rubber shelf liner from sticking to your presser foot while sewing, sew through **strips of notebook paper.**

8

Once the rubber shelf liner is securely attached to the felt at all four sides, carefully remove and discard the paper.

9

Sew bottom square onto the rest of the felt body, using a
¹/₂" seam allowance, stopping ¹/₂" from the top and bottom
of edges and backstitching to secure each seam.

Your glued foam cube will now measure 18" x 18" x 18".
Gently ease felt slipcover over foam cube until it's snug.

10

Using **FoamFast 74 spray adhesive,** attach two pieces of
6" thick high-density foam that have been cut to 18"
square. Then attach one piece of **6" thick medium-density
foam** cut 18" square to the top of the stack.

Turn cube over and close bottom by pressing
Velcro strips together.

11

12

E A S E
LEVEL
1

TWO-TONE AREA RUG

Dynamic special effects take place under foot when you combine two different textures of carpet tile. Here, we used the high-traffic fuzzy kind to create a border around our smoother olive-toned tiles. Incidentally, borders help define and enhance any space, whether it's large or not-so-large. Plus, you can easily change the carpet to match your mood: As in the Sweet Dreams Suit, we used carpet tiles with a low-tack adhesive that's easy to lift and switch.

1

Define the interior size of your area rug by placing **low-pile carpet tiles (InterfaceFLOR Solid Ground in Palm 882510)** in the desired area of the room from the center out. Sticking the interior tiles to the floor isn't necessary, since the adhered border tiles will secure the rug in place.

2

Create a frame for the area rug with one row of **shaggy deep pile carpet tiles in a contrasting color (InterfaceFLOR "Housepet" in Parakeet 609006).**

3

Complete the rug by laying in the corner pieces last. Adjust placement of rug if necessary, and secure corner tiles only by peeling and sticking the adhesive backs.

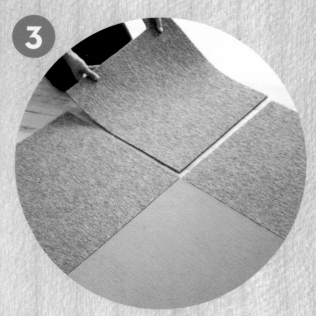

CUBBY CREDENZA

EASE
LEVEL
3

This modular bookcase comes to life when adorned with mismatched "veneer" detailing—more of the same fun, mod marquetry we learned how to create earlier. Options are illustrated on pages 164 and 165. The doors keep what's behind them safely dust-free (especially handy for CDs and DVDs), while the asymmetrically placed door handles keep the atmosphere in your reading room playful and inviting.

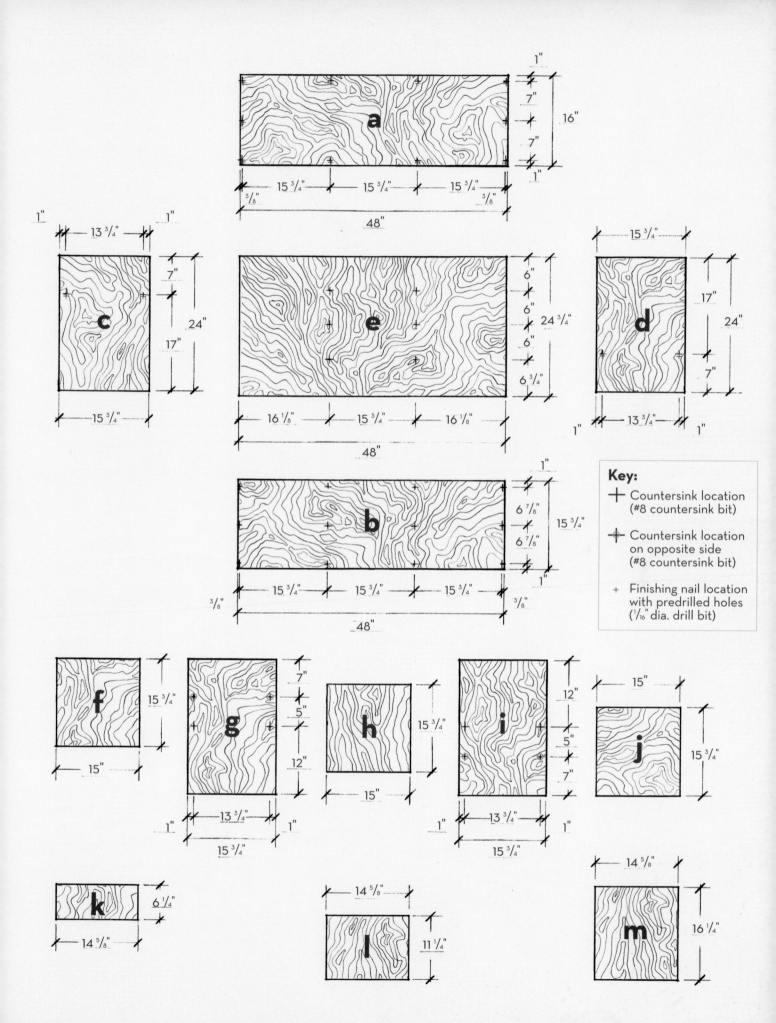

Key:

✛ Countersink location (#8 countersink bit)

✛ Countersink location on opposite side (#8 countersink bit)

+ Finishing nail location with predrilled holes (¹/₁₆" dia. drill bit)

1 Cut, predrill, sand, stain, and finish all wood pieces as noted in blueprint. Using **1 1/4" drywall screws,** attach two center supports (g) and (i) to bottom piece (b).

2 Mark placement for center shelf (h) 11 5/8" up and attach through center supports (g) and (i) using 1 1/4" drywall scre

3 Attach two side pieces (c) and (d) to base (b) of assembly with 1 1/4" drywall screws.

4 Mark placement for right side shelf (j) 6 5/8" up and attach to center support (h) using 1 1/4" drywall screws.

5 Secure shelf (j) to outside piece (d) using **1 1/2" finishing nails,** being careful not to the ding the wood with your **hammer.**

6 Mark placement for left side shelf (f) 16 5/8" up and attach as noted in steps 4 and 5.

7 Run a bead of **wood glue** along top edge of vertical supports. Carefully place top piece (a) onto construction and align.

8 Secure top piece (a) with 1 1/2" finishing nails, through all vertical supports.

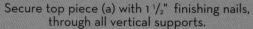

9 Attach ¾" **pipe flanges** to bottom piece (b) at all 4 corners, using ¾" **screws.**

10 Secure **rubber tips** to 4" x ¾" pipe legs.

11 Screw all four legs into flanges, tightening until secure.

12 With cabinet face down, run a bead of wood glue on all upright surfaces. Carefully place back piece (e) onto construction and align.

13 Secure back to construction using 1 ½" finishing nails along edge.

14 Cut **piano hinges** for doors, as noted in blueprint, using a **hacksaw.** Mark your cut line with **masking tape** and **clamp** hinge to a table before sawing.

15 Attach piano hinge to door (k) using the screws that came with your hinge. Repeat steps 14–16 for other doors (l) and (m).

16 Attach hinged door (k) to outside edge of upper left cubby hole using the screws that came with your hinge. If door is difficult to close, sand wood or realign door

The easiest of our veneer work, this regiment stripe is simply a **2" wide piece of light wood** with a **contrasting 1" wide strip** centered on top.

This wooden cobblestone effect is achieved by cutting out circles in a **variety of sizes and wood tones.**

1

Measure and mark 2" stripes onto a light colored self-stick wood veneer.

1

Draw or trace circle shapes on backside of **self-stick wood veneer.**

2

For a sharp edge, carefully cut using an **X-Acto blade** and a **metal edged ruler.**

2

Cut out circles using **heavy duty metal scissors.**

3

Cut 1" wide contrasting strip, peel off adhesive back and adhere on center of 2" strip. Repeat and adhere completed stripes to door face.

3

Begin applying wooden cobblestones in a random order. Cut straight edges on some circles for edge application, as shown.

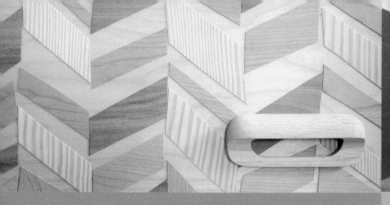

This stuttered-chevron design looks ultramodern with a contrasting lozenge-shaped door handle.

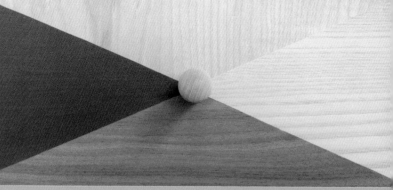

For these pennant shaped quadrants, you'll need three different wood veneers. The fourth quadrant is the face of the door.

1 Measure and mark 2" stripes on the back of a piece of wood veneer. Draw angled lines as shown, in different widths.

1 Make a pattern piece that is the exact size of your door. Draw two lines from corner to corner.

2 For a crisp edge, cut out pieces using an **X-Acto blade** and a **metal edged ruler.**

2 Cut along lines and trace one pattern piece onto each of three colors of wood veneer.

3 Begin applying angled strips along one side, staggering the space between each strip. Reverse angle on next row of strips to create a chevron.

3 Cut out and apply, matching all veneer points at the center of the door. Attach a round drawer pull at intersection.

PHOTO LAMP

EASE
2
LEVEL

Memories light the corners of your mind; now they can illuminate your rooms as well. Printed on Mylar and backed with heavyweight plastic, photographs new and old are unforgettable treasures and functional keepsakes.

1

o create the lampshade form, cut out a iece of **heavy duty frosted plastic** that measures 24" tall x 32 ¹/₂" wide.

2

Print an image onto **backlight computer paper.** Piece smaller images together if necessary, cut to same size as plastic and adhere with spray adhesive.

3

Mark holes for center back seam starting ¹/₄" down from the top and ¹/₄" in from side at 3" intervals. Repeat on opposing side.

4

unch holes at marked locations using a **holepunch.** Repeat on other side.

5

Bring both sides together and overlap, matching up holes. Insert **brass brads** into holes and secure.

6

Drill a ³/₈" hole into a **10" round disk,** 2" from outside edge, for electrical cord. Insert a ³/₈" x **1" metal nipple.** Attach **four brass upholstery tacks** as lamp feet into bottom of wood plaque.

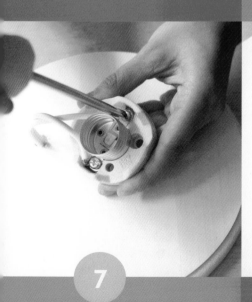

7

Insert an **electrical cord** through the bottom of the plaque. Strip cord, and tach positive and negative wires to the screws on a porcelain lamp base.

8

Screw lamp base into center of wood plaque using ³/₄" **screws.**

9

Slide plastic tube over wood plaque and with a **hammer,** secure with brass upholstery tacks all the way around.

STRIPED WALL

EASE
LEVEL
2

The most rewarding thing about painting decorative stripes on your walls is that when you're done, you've achieved instant, big-top success, converting boring solid-color walls into a vibrant, circus-happy canvas that's guaranteed to inspire you every time you look at it. Vertical stripes have an amazing telescoping effect. Even a low-ceilinged room feels taller and more exalting when it's decked out in sharp, vertical stripes. Painting is a snap, as you'll see—just remember to be patient between coats and let the paint dry all the way, or your eagerness could end up blurring the lines!

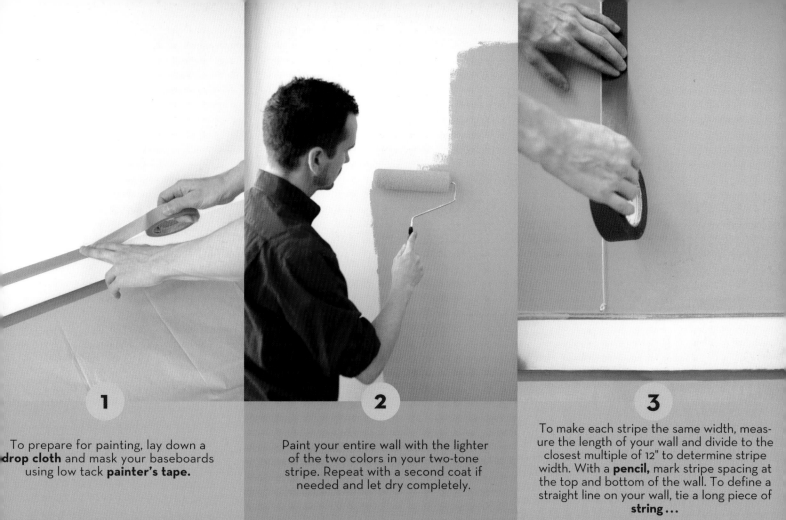

1

To prepare for painting, lay down a **drop cloth** and mask your baseboards using low tack **painter's tape.**

2

Paint your entire wall with the lighter of the two colors in your two-tone stripe. Repeat with a second coat if needed and let dry completely.

3

To make each stripe the same width, measure the length of your wall and divide to the closest multiple of 12" to determine stripe width. With a **pencil,** mark stripe spacing at the top and bottom of the wall. To define a straight line on your wall, tie a long piece of **string . . .**

. . . around a **pushpin** and insert at pencil mark near the ceiling. Pull string taut and tie to a second push pin that is inserted at bottom pencil mark. To mask the outsides of the stripe, follow along the outside of the string line with a piece of painter's tape. Continue for each stripe.

Once all the stripes are masked, carefully paint in darker stripe color, making sure to keep within the tape lines. Repeat with a second coat of paint if necessary.

Let paint dry completely, and remove painter's tape, by gently pulling in an angled downward motion as shown.

4

5

6

CURATOR SHELF

EASE
LEVEL
2

This is a wonderful way to go about displaying all your pretties, whether you collect boxes of Cheerios or first-edition paperbacks from the 1950s—or both. After all, showing off collectibles is the best part of getting, keeping, and dusting them—and these handsome shelves turn even novice collectors into polished art curators without annihilating every last inch of wall space. And when your collecting feelers branch out (as they are bound to do), these versatile shelves will enable you to rotate your installations, just like they do in galleries and museums, to reflect your passion du jour.

Attach two pieces of **1" x 6" clear pine** cut to the desired length of your shelf together with **wood glue.**

1

2 Secure with **1 1/4" finishing nails,** alternating sides at 8" intervals.

Cut a piece of **2 1/4" lattice** to the length of your shelf and secure to shelf face with wood glue and 1 1/4" finishing nails.

3

4 Attach **2 1/2" L brackets** with 1 1/4" drywall **screws,** every 18".

Attach shelf to wall using appropriate **heavy-duty wall anchors** through L brackets.

5

DAILY SPECIAL

Just as headline news changes every day, so does the information you need to keep handy. This felt-covered bulletin board, with charmingly coordinated pushpins, lets you be the editor *and* the art director.

1

Cut a leaf pattern out of **paper** and trace onto two pieces of **wool felt.** Cut the stem off one of the leaves.

2

Insert a **T-pin** through the stemmed leaf as shown, making sure not to pierce through to the front of the felt.

3

Apply a thin layer of **fabric glue** to the backside of the stemmed leaf.

4

Gently place back piece onto glued area, sealing pin in place.

5

Cut a small strip out of a contrasting color of wool felt to make the leaf vein.

6

Apply felt vein with fabric glue, using a pin to press it into place if necessary.

7

Mask all the edges of a **premade cork-board** with **painter's tape.** Lay board onto a **drop cloth** in a well ventilated area.

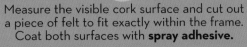

8

Measure the visible cork surface and cut out a piece of felt to fit exactly within the frame. Coat both surfaces with **spray adhesive.**

9

Adhere felt piece to cork and remove tape from frame. Attach a picture with the leaf pins, and enjoy!

CHARLES
HARPER

I first encountered the exquisite work of Charles Harper in vintage '50s-era issues of a lifestyle magazine called *Ford Times*, published by the Ford Motor Company. His illustrations were so charming and compelling, and somehow they also felt very familiar to me, although I didn't know exactly why. Ever since, I've been voraciously scooping up anything and everything signed by Charles Harper, especially prints depicting flora and fauna (his bird drawings are among my favorites).

Along the way, I figured out where I'd seen his work before: In my favorite childhood book, *The Giant Golden Book of Biology*. First published in 1961, that book was incredibly formative for me, and Charles Harper's illustrations are the reason why. They're the reason I've always been—and always will be—fascinated with science and animals. With his deft drawings and dynamic color sense, he made everything riveting, whether the topic was insect genesis or human musculature. Educational, exciting, tickling, his illustrations facilitated the easy assimilation of advanced information. He shaped my mind and thrilled me into learning.

Nobody else can render molecule-splitting the way Charles Harper can! On his sketchpad, a simple sugar molecule becomes a dazzling pattern of persimmon, brown-black, and burnt-olive dots. His sensibilities and color combinations mirror the mid-century modern textiles I'm crazy about. With just a few delicate strokes, he implies everything there is to know about his subject, no matter how vast or how microscopic, from atoms to astronomy. And his wonderful sense of humor is apparent in the witty titles he hangs on his works: "Crabitat" . . . "Herondipity" . . . "Family Owlbum" . . . "Raccoonnaissance."

"I don't count the feathers; I count the wings," the artist once said. Thankfully, Charles Harper sorted it all out, so our imaginations could fly free.

STENCIL
PAINTING

EASE
LEVEL
2

Inspired by the art of Charles Harper, this faux silkscreen is easy to create using Con-Tact Brand paper, spray paint, and—for that Handmade Modern touch—dappled paint applied with scrunched-up plastic bags.

1

Make a pompom stamp out of a **plastic grocery bag** by folding it as shown and securing one end with a **rubber band.**

2

Trim ends with **pinking shears** and fluff the plastic into a ball

3

Dip pompom into watered down **acrylic paint** and begin stamping onto a **pre-stretched canvas.** Continue stamping until the entire canvas is mottled with paint.

4

Trace canvas onto a piece of **Con-Tact Brand paper** and cut ou

5

Cut a large leaf shape out of **paper** and trace onto the canvas sized Con-Tact Brand paper.

6

Cut out leaf stencil, saving inside piece for a later step. Stick Co Tact Brand paper to canvas, making sure leaf shape is centered

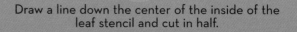

7

pray a fine layer of **light green spray paint** over stencil, making sure to work in a well-ventilated area.

8

Draw a line down the center of the inside of the leaf stencil and cut in half.

9

tick leaf half onto canvas, shifting up ½" from the leaf shape that as already been painted, to create an "off register" effect. Spray lightly over canvas with a **darker shade of green spray paint.**

10

Let paint dry completely and carefully remove all stencil pieces from canvas.

11

Cut out varied lengths of **cardboard** to use as stamps for the leaf veins. Dip the edge of the cardboard into a **shallow tray of brown acrylic paint.**

12

Stamp the cardboard onto the canvas to create the veins on your leaf. Use a 4" piece stamped end on end to create middle vein.

179

STRING ART

The first time I ever saw art incorporating string was on a trip to an art museum, when I was a boy, where I was amazed with works by the Russian-born Constructivist sculptor Naum Gabo. I was excited that I had the same things in my garage as a famous artist had in his! String art is so modern and graphic, yet it also has wonderfully nostalgic references to Spirograph and Jacob's Ladder—and the variations are delightfully, mind-bogglingly endless.

1 Place a piece of **20" x 20" x ³/₄" plywood** onto a piece of **colored burlap** that is 26" x 26".

2 Attach with a **staple gun,** folding over the edges twice to hide the raw edge. Go back and forth from one side of the plywood to the other as you staple it down, to create even tension.

3 Rotate wood a quarter turn and continue stapling on other sides.

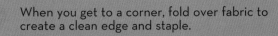

4 When you get to a corner, fold over fabric to create a clean edge and staple.

5 Cut two 8 ½" x 18" rectangles out of **graph paper** and mark with dots that are ¾" apart and ½" in from the edge.

Place both rectangles of paper onto the front of your burlap-covered piece of wood, making sure they are lined up and equally spaced.

6

7 Attach graph paper with ¾" **copper and/or brass plated nails,** hammering one through each dot. Once all nails are in, remove paper from board.

Tie one end of **yarn** around the nail in the bottom left-hand corner of one of the rectangles. Wind the yarn around the nail in the top right-hand corner and bring back to the bottom left-hand corner, wrapping it around the nail right above the first nail.

8

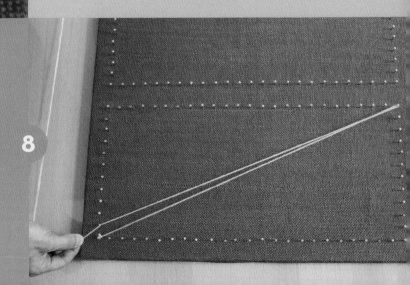

9 Continue going back and forth from corner to corner, shifting clockwise to the next nail as you wind.

As your shape begins to take form, extra dimension may be added by pushing the string up or down on the nails. **10**

11 Continue wrapping as shown, making sure to keep yarn taut.

Once you wrap back around to your starter nail, secure yarn with a double slip knot and a small bit of **glue.** **12**

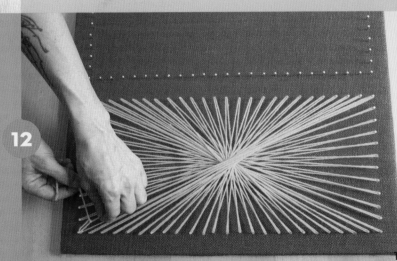

TICK TOCK WALL CLOCK

EASE
LEVEL
2

Wooden coffee stirrers can do more than mix milk and sugar into your morning java; they can actually measure time. That's precisely what they're doing on this timepiece, which uses the humble little sticks as hands. As for the dramatic, op-art clock face in deep greens and blues, well . . . the very concept of time is kaleidoscopic, so why not celebrate that with a kaleidoscope pattern?

1 On a **16" x 16" x 1 ½" canvas,** draw pencil lines from corner to corner with a **ruler** to find the center.

2 Divide the canvas into 12 equally sized wedges by dividing each side into thirds and drawing straight lines with your ruler. Continue all lines off the side of the canvas.

3 Mask off one wedge at a time with **painter's tape** and paint in wedge with **acrylic paint** and a **small paintbrush.** Let dry completely before removing tape.

4 Continue masking off and painting in other wedges with varying shades of **green and blue acrylic paint.**

5 Once the entire canvas is painted, pierce a small hole in the center of the canvas with an **X-Acto blade.**

6 Enlarge the hole with a pencil until it is big enough for the top of a **2" clock mechanism** to fit through.

7

Cut out two 2 ¼" **foam core** squares that are the same size as your clock mechanism. Punch a hole through the center of each square, using a pencil.

8

Tidy up foam core punctures by gently pushing any paper that has poked through back into the hole to reduce bulk.

9

To determine the length of the 2 ¼" wide foam core support piece for the clock mechanism, measure and mark the distance between the wood canvas supports. Add 1 ¼" to either end and cut out. Find the center point by drawing straight lines from corner to corner.

10

Punch a hole in the foam core at the center point using a pencil.

11

Being careful not to cut all the way through, lightly score the foam core 1 ¼" from each end.

12

Apply two strips of **double stick mounting tape** to the front of the clock mechanism.

Layer the three pieces of foam core as shown, matching up center holes. Secure together with glue or tape, and insert clock mechanism through holes.

13

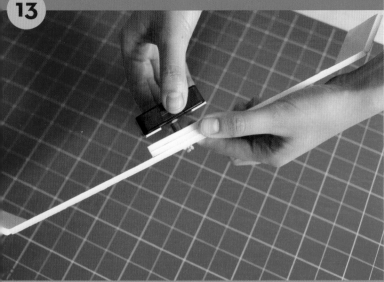

Fold up scored edges of foam core assembly, and place into the back of your canvas, making sure the clock pokes all the way through to the front of the canvas.

14

Apply double stick mounting tape to the folded ends of the support piece and secure against the frame of the canvas.

15

Carefully apply **super glue gel** to the metal hands of your clock.

16

Attach metal hands to **raw wood coffee stirrers**, clipping one stirrer down a little shorter to create the hour hand.

17

Assemble the hands onto the clock mechanism, following the instructions on the package. Finish by attaching the second hand as shown.

18

RUSSEL + MARY WRIGHT

The uniquely American lifestyle promoted by Russel and Mary Wright continues to set a fine example for contemporary living that's gracious yet casual. The title of their book, *Guide to Easier Living*, sums up their philosophy. Notice the Wrights didn't try to pull our legs by saying it's easy; they offered genuinely helpful tips to make it eas*ier*. And their designs were as realistic and un-stuffy as they were.

In matters of lifestyle, the Wrights always placed the emphasis on life. Nowhere is this more evident, I think, than in Russel's designs for Iroquois China. This was fine china you were not afraid to handle and really use. I'll never forget the image of the couple demonstrating their china's durability by swiftly overturning a full dish rack and trying—unsuccessfully—to break the contents! No wonder so many people continue to collect vintage Wright china; unlike most collectibles, these pieces can happily be used precisely the way the designer intended them to be used: on a daily basis.

To me, the china's organic shapes almost seem inspired by mole-cules or amoebas, all in the most beautiful colors. Russel Wright was a genius colorist, offering rich palettes of sky blue, mocha, flesh, and chartreuse. Perfect in combinations or on their own, I'm sure everything tastes better on this china!

Plus, the silhouettes are so lovely to look at, with their long, sensual, curving handles. Russel Wright's china appears delicate, but it's actually the most sturdy stuff: mine goes right in the dishwasher. The designs he created for Melmac really are unbreakable, and they came in brilliant pool blue; beautiful coral; bright, buttery yellow; taupe; chocolate; red ... their patina ever richer now, after over fifty years of use.

Bring a Russel Wright covered casserole to the table and you get instant drama in the presentation of your dish—what a nice reward for working in the kitchen. The Wrights celebrated dining and entertaining, whether you were eating alone, dining à deux, or having guests over. They knew how to entertain because they *were* entertainers, and there's a delightful sense of ritual in everything they did.

SMOKESTACK LAMP

Act like a magpie in the hardware store—reach for this radiator grate and that drawer pull, add in a sheet of heavyweight plastic—and you'll come up with all the misappropriated elements needed to fabricate this stylish light source!

Divide a **10" wood disk** into quadrants with a **ruler.** Mark and predrill leg holes on quadrant lines ³/₄" in from outside edge. At center mark, drill one ³/₈" hole for the socket support.

1

Attach **four silver drawer pulls** to the bottom of the wood disk to create the legs of your lamp.

2

Use a 12" piece of ³/₈" **all-thread** for the **light socket** support. Thread a ¹/₂" **metal sleeve** onto the all-thread.

3

Insert all-thread into center hole on the wood disk and secure with a **nut** on the bottom side.

4

5 Cut the end off of an unplugged **extension cord** and feed through the all-thread from the base toward the socket.

6 Screw socket base to top of all-thread and gently separate top of socket from base to expose wiring screws.

7 Split and strip extension cord and carefully secure positive and negative wires to the light socket.

8 Pull wire taut and push top of socket back into base.

Trim a **perforated metal radiator grill** to 32 ¹/₂" x 36" with **metal snips.**

9

Form the grill into a cylinder by over-lapping 1" and connecting with **¹/₂" pan head bolts, washers, and nuts** approximately every 6" (seven total).

10

Slide cylinder over lamp base and attach around the edges with **1" pan head screws.**

11

Cut a sheet of **frosted heavyweight plastic** 31 ¹/₂" x 18" and insert into the tube. Screw a **40-watt frosted aquarium lightbulb** into the socket.

12

193

TINY TABLEAUX TABLES

EASE LEVEL 1

For a vibrant decorative jolt, color-xerox your favorite pattern, from houndstooth to horticulture, and lay it on the table—literally!

1

Cut out two pieces of **³/₄" plywood** that measure 12" x 18". Secure one on top of the other with **wood glue.**

2

Coat short ends of table with **Mod Podge.** Cover with two 2" x 13" pieces of **printed paper,** dipping in **water** before applying.

3

Cover with another layer of Mod Podge, folding excess paper over the top. Miter the corners and fold in before applying the two 2" x 18" pieces to other sides.

4

Cut out a top piece of paper that measures 12" x 18". Apply to tabletop and coat with two layers of Mod Podge.

5

Once the tabletop is completely dry, flip it over and install **pre-made hairpin legs** in the corners.

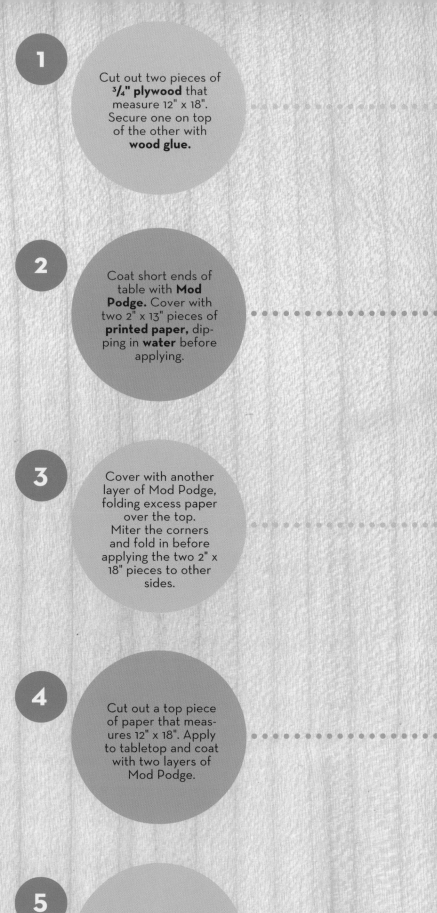

ALEXANDER GIRARD

Alexander Girard wants YOU to have a nice day!

Well, he might not have actually said that, but it's clearly the message conveyed by the relentlessly joyful work of this pioneering designer who's been such a hero to me.

I recently had the pleasure of visiting the Museum of International Folk Art in Santa Fe, repository of the world's most important collection of folk art. Girard and his wife Susan amassed over 100,000 handmade objects, the vibrant, whimsical work of folk artisans from around the globe. Often, modernism comes across as cold and hard; Girard made it colorful, warm, and inviting by taking cues from the folk art he loved. It's clear that what so impassioned him about these artifacts was their human touch: it's evident in every single piece in this astonishing collection.

For Girard, an interior was about "seeing, touching, and remembering familiar associations and all the other intangible activities of the mind and soul." Mostly, we think of those "intangible activities" taking place in private, at home. But isn't inspiration just as vital in public spaces, for instance, at the office?

As director of textile design for Herman Miller, which supplied so many fabrics for corporate environments, Girard helped to make the American workplace almost a home away from home with brightly colored, boldly patterned contract fabrics for chairs and partitions. The beautiful bravery of his palette is unparalleled, and the scale of his patterns is so charming. He's among the few textile designers whose work has never dated. These fabrics were so gorgeous, they managed to infuse machine-made automation with a handmade, artisanal feel. Just imagine how productive you'd be, how many new ideas you'd get, if your task chair was covered in exuberant fuchsia Mikado fabric, a geometric floral inspired by the sensual, traditional textiles of Japan.

And why shouldn't the warm, soft feelings of home surround us on our travels too? That was Girard's thinking as he was approached by Braniff International in 1965, when he redesigned everything from the ticket counters and airplane interiors to the luggage tags, blankets, and playing cards. Watching the planes take off was especially fun, as Girard had specified that the fuselage be spray-painted in brilliant shades of blue, orange, turquoise, and yellow. He created Braniff's colors, then literally flew them sky-high.

Growing up in Texas in the '60s, I saw a lot of the Dallas–Fort Worth Braniff terminal, and like the millions of other Americans who flew Braniff, I got a delightful, unforgettable immersion course in modernism. Today, one of the sofas from those terminal lounges occupies pride of place in my home away from home, my design studio. With its molded-wood-and-plastic frame and green-blue striped upholstery, it still looks fresh. It's a constant and welcome reminder of the genius of Alexander Girard.

EASE
3
LEVEL

When landscaping the Great Indoors, it's a challenge to keep plants off the floor, where they inevitably cause water damage to rugs and wood parquet. This planter uses jewel-toned aquarium gravel, which not only looks dazzling, it also holds moisture so you won't need to water plants as frequently. The bench, meanwhile, is quite versatile: the velour-covered seat cushion pops right off for use as a floor cushion. Pull it up to the wooden seat, which doubles neatly as a floor desk!

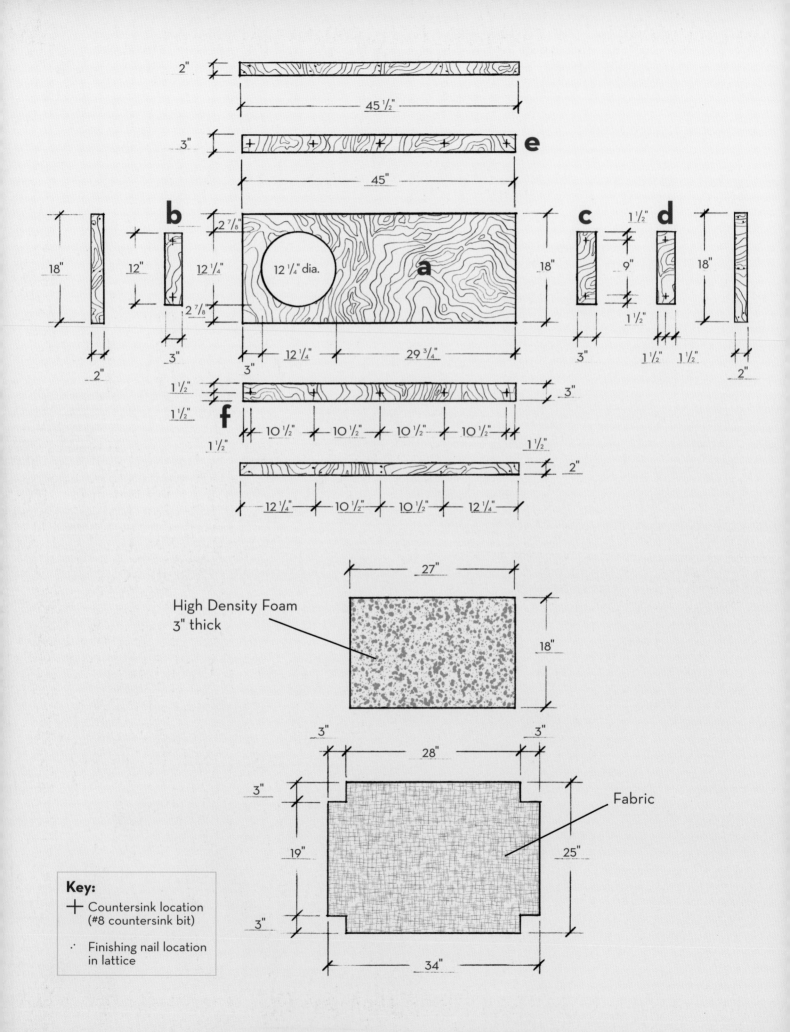

2"

45 ½"

3"   **e**

45"

b   2 ⅞"

18"   12"   12 ¼"   12 ¼" dia.   **a**   18"   **c**   1 ½"   **d**   18"

2 ⅞"   9"

2"   3"   3"   12 ¼"   29 ¾"   3"   1 ½"   1 ½"   2"

1 ½"   3"

1 ½"   **f**

1 ½"   10 ½"   10 ½"   10 ½"   10 ½"   1 ½"

2"

12 ¼"   10 ½"   10 ½"   12 ¼"

27"

High Density Foam
3" thick   18"

3"   28"   3"

3"

Fabric

19"   25"

3"

34"

Key:
+ Countersink location
   (#8 countersink bit)

· Finishing nail location
   in lattice

1 Cut and sand all wood pieces as shown in the blueprint. Draw a 16" square at the left end of the ply-wood bench seat (a), and find the center point using a **ruler.**

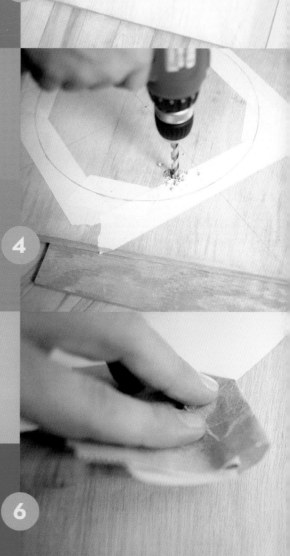

2 Draw a 12" circle in the center of the square by making a compass using a **piece of string** tied around a **pushpin.** Tie a **pencil** to the other end of the string, 6" from the pushpin. Keeping the string taut, draw the circumference of your circle.

3 To prevent the wood from splinter-ing during cutting, cover the circle with **masking tape** and retrace.

4 To cleanly insert the saw blade into the wood, drill a 3/4" pilot hole 1 1/2" in from the side of your pencil line.

5 Insert **jigsaw** blade into pilot hole and begin cutting out the 12" circle, care-fully following along the pencil line.

6 Remove tape and sand down edges with **80 grit sandpaper.**

7 Attach outside braces (e) and (f) to long sides on the bottom of the plat-form with **wood glue.**

8 Measure and mark a center line on the bottom of the platform and attach center brace (c) with wood glue. Attach end braces (b) and (d) in same manner.

9 Reinforce all braces with **1 ¼" drywall screws.**

10 Before attaching side lattice panels, drive **1 ¼" finishing nails** every 8" partially in the wood for easier handling.

11 Line up the top of each lattice piece so it is flush with the top of the bench, and attach with 1 ¼" finishing nails.

12 Flip over platform and attach **¾" pipe flanges** at each corner of the bench with 1 ¼" drywall screws.

13 Slide a **rubber cap** over one end of each of the **four 14" pipe legs.**

14 Screw pipe legs into the flanges at all four corners. Set bench upright on pipe legs and stain with **Minwax water-based stain in Wild Berry.** Coat all visible wood surfaces with **polyurethane.**

15 For the cushion, cut the pattern specified on the blueprint out of **heavyweight paper,** and trace onto **a piece of fabric** as shown.

16 For the zippered base of the cushion, cut out two bottom pieces as specified on the blueprint.

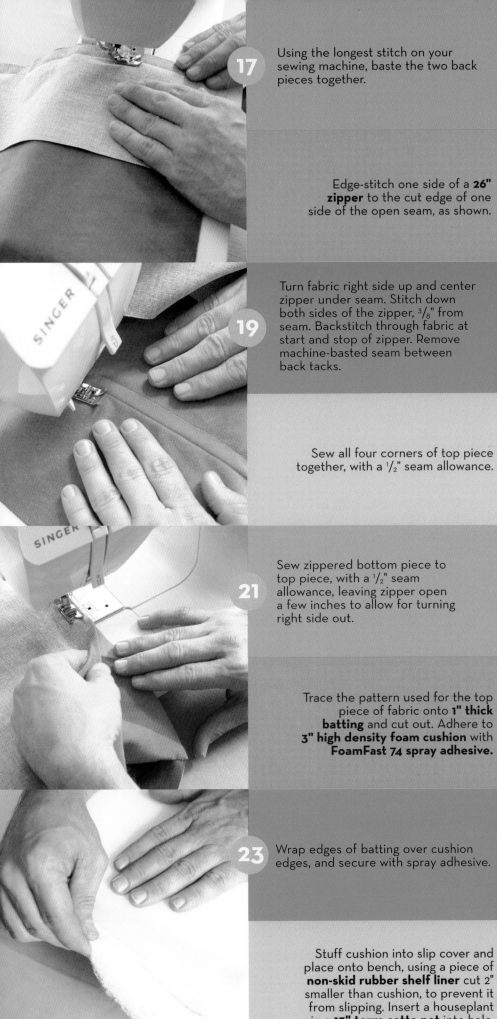

17 Using the longest stitch on your sewing machine, baste the two back pieces together.

Edge-stitch one side of a **26" zipper** to the cut edge of one side of the open seam, as shown. **18**

19 Turn fabric right side up and center zipper under seam. Stitch down both sides of the zipper, $^3/_8$" from seam. Backstitch through fabric at start and stop of zipper. Remove machine-basted seam between back tacks.

Sew all four corners of top piece together, with a $^1/_2$" seam allowance. **20**

21 Sew zippered bottom piece to top piece, with a $^1/_2$" seam allowance, leaving zipper open a few inches to allow for turning right side out.

Trace the pattern used for the top piece of fabric onto **1" thick batting** and cut out. Adhere to **3" high density foam cushion** with **FoamFast 74 spray adhesive**. **22**

23 Wrap edges of batting over cushion edges, and secure with spray adhesive.

Stuff cushion into slip cover and place onto bench, using a piece of **non-skid rubber shelf liner** cut 2" smaller than cushion, to prevent it from slipping. Insert a houseplant in a **13" terra cotta pot** into hole. **24**

Alexander Girard Designs for Herman Miller by Leslie Piña; Schiffer Publishing Ltd., 1998

An Eames Primer by Eames Demetrios; Universe Publishing, 2002

Beguiled by the Wild: The Art of Charley Harper by Charley Harper; Flower Valley Press, 1995

Case Study Houses by Elizabeth Smith and Peter Goessel; Taschen, 2002

Eva Zeisel by Lucie Young, Marisa Bartolucci and Raul Cabra; Chronicle Books, 2003

Eva Zeisel on Design by Eva Zeisel; Overlook Press, March 2004

George Nelson: The Design of Modern Design by Stanley Abercrombie; The MIT Press, 1995

Isamu Noguchi: A Study of Space by Ana Maria Torres; Monacelli Press, 2000

Julius Shulman: Architecture and Its Photography by Julius Shulman and Peter Gossel; Taschen, 1998

Knoll Furniture, 1938–1960 by Steven and Linda Rouland; Schiffer Publishing Ltd., 1999

Mary and Russel Wright's Guide to Easier Living by Mary and Russel Wright; Gibbs Smith Publishers, 2003

Nature Form & Spirit: The Life and Legacy of George Nakashima by Mira Nakashima; Harry N. Abrams, 2003

Ralph Rapson: Sixty Years of Modern Design by Jane King Hession, Rip Rapson and Bruce N. Wright; Afton Historical Society Press, 1999

Russel Wright: Creating American Lifestyle by Donald Albrecht and Robert Schonfeld; Harry N. Abrams, 2001

The Soul of a Tree: A Woodworker's Reflections by George Nakashima; Kodansha America; Reprint edition 1988

Work of Charles and Ray Eames by Donald Albrecht; Harry N. Abrams, 1997

SUGGESTED READING

Con-Tact Brand—for self-stick shelf paper; www.contactbrand.com

Design Within Reach—one-stop midcentury design resource; www.dwr.com

Dick Blick—art store megasite; www.dickblick.com

Ebay—online auction house; www.ebay.com

Feltpro—for wool felt; www.feltpro.net

Fred Soll Incense—for handmade incense; www.fredsoll.com

Hobbylinc.com—for glass test tubes; www.hobbylinc.com

Home Depot—hardware megasite; www.homedepot.com

InterfaceFLOR—for carpet tiles; www.interfaceflor.com

Kate's Paperie—for handmade papers; www.katespaperie.com

Knoll Museum—open by appointment only; reservations call 215-679-1388

Lowe's—hardware megasite; www.lowes.com

Michael's—arts and crafts megasite; www.michaels.com

Modernica—original and reproduction midcentury furniture; www.modernica.net

MoMA Online Store—for modern masterpieces and books; www.momastore.org

Pearl Paint—art store megasite; www.pearlpaint.com

Père Furniture—for hairpin legs; http://stores.andale.com/perelogo

Replacements, Ltd.—for Russel Wright tableware; www.replacements.com

Rockler—for pressure sensitive (self-stick) wood veneer; www.rockler.com

Waddell Manufacturing—for wooden table legs; www.waddellmfg.com

Wright—online auction house for midcentury masterpieces; www.wright20.com

CUT LISTS

Part 1—Sofa Bench . . . page 24

³/₄" Birch Veneer Plywood
1 piece at 40 ³/₄" x 48"
2 pieces at 40 ³/₄" x 29"
1 piece at 24 ³/₄" x 48"
2 pieces at 23" x 28 ³/₄"
1 piece at 20" x 48"
1 piece at 13 ¹/₂" x 48"
1 piece at 13 ¹/₂" x 46 ¹/₂"
1 piece at 9" x 46 ¹/₂"
1 piece at 9" x 24"
2 pieces at 3 ¹/₂" x 46"
2 pieces at 3 ¹/₂" x 37"
8 pieces at 3 ¹/₂" x 3 ¹/₂"

1 ¹/₂" x 30" Piano Hinges
2 pieces cut to 28 ³/₄"

4" High Density Foam
1 piece at 48" x 20"
1 piece at 48" x 20"

6 yards of 46" wide Fabric

Part 2—Floating Boxes and Trim . . . page 28

³/₄" Birch Veneer Plywood
2 pieces at 12" x 44"
2 pieces at 12" x 40"
2 pieces at 12" x 28"
6 pieces at 12" x 12"
6 pieces at 6" x 6"

1 ³/₄" diameter Conduit
2 pieces cut to desired length

¹/₂" diameter Aluminum Rod
6 pieces cut to 4" each

Illuminated End Table . . . page 58 (Set of 2)

³/₄" Birch Veneer Plywood
2 pieces at 28" x 32"
4 pieces at 10 ¹/₄" x 32"
4 pieces at 10 ¹/₄" x 26 ¹/₂"

¹/₂" Plexiglass
2 pieces at 28" x 32"

1 ³/₄" diameter Conduit
8 pieces at 16 ¹/₄"
8 pieces at 1 ¹/₂"

¹/₄" x 1¹/₂" Fender Washers (8 total)
⁵/₁₆" x 2" Fender Washers (16 total)
¹/₄" x 3" Lag Bolts (8 total)

Daybed Library . . . page 66

³/₄" Birch Veneer Plywood
1 piece at 29 ¹/₂" x 57 ³/₄"
1 piece at 16" x 56 ¹/₄"
2 pieces at 11 ¹/₄" x 29 ¹/₂"
1 piece at 11 ¹/₄" x 56 ¹/₄"
1 piece at 8 ¹/₂" x 16"
1 piece at 2" x 56 ¹/₄"

Daybed Library Upholstery

4" High Density Foam
1 piece at 57" x 29"
1 piece at 57" x 12"

Fabric and Batting:
2 yards aqua velveteen
4 yards striped fabric
4 yards of 1" thick batting

Corduroy Ottoman . . . page 20

³/₄" AC Plywood
1 piece at 30" diameter

4 Wooden Legs (Waddell #2658)

4 Straight Braces (Waddell #2751)

2" High Density Foam
1 piece at 30" diameter

2" Low Density Foam
1 piece at 30" diameter

Fabric and Batting:
1 yard cocoa corduroy
1 yard aqua corduroy
1 yard of 1" thick batting

Knock-Out Room Divider . . . page 52

³/₈" AC Plywood
2 pieces at 30" x 34"

³/₄" Birch Plywood
12 pieces at 6" x 6"

1 ³/₄" diameter Conduit
2 pieces cut to desired length

Storage Bench . . . page 90

3/4" Birch Veneer Plywood
2 pieces at 16" x 48"
1 piece at 16" x 47 3/4"
2 pieces at 16" x 5"
2 pieces at 15 1/4" x 5"
1 piece at 5" x 16 1/2"

4 Wooden Legs (Waddell #2506)

4 Angle Braces (Waddell #2752)

4" High Density Foam
1 piece at 48" x 16"

Fabric and Batting:
2 yards of 48" wide vinyl
2 yards of 1" thick batting

Illuminated Wood Tile Headboard . . . page 98

3/8" AC Plywood
2 pieces at 29" x 81"
16 pieces at 16" x 16"
2 pieces at 16" x 20"
2 pieces at 20" x 16"

1" x 4" Pine Frame
2 pieces at 77 5/8"
1 piece at 52 3/4"
2 pieces at 51 1/4"
2 pieces at 24"

2" x 4" Ledger
1 piece at 51"

2 packs of 20' long Rope Lights

Beauty Station . . . page 84

3/4" Birch Veneer Plywood
2 pieces at 16" x 36"
2 pieces at 16" x 3 1/2"
1 piece at 3 1/2" x 34 1/2"

4 Wooden Legs (Waddell #2528)

4 Angle Braces (Waddell #2752)

3 1/2" Diameter Aluminum Cups
3 total

Floating Bed Platform . . . page 102

3/4" Birch Veneer Plywood
2 pieces at 31" x 81"
2 pieces at 40 1/2" x 62"

1 5/8" Lattice (1/4" thick)
2 pieces at 81"
1 piece at 62 1/2"

3/4" Black Pipe Flanges
9 pieces total

3/4" Threaded Black Pipe
9 pieces at 8" long

Bedside Library . . . page 114
(Set of 2)

3/4" Birch Veneer Plywood
4 pieces at 14" x 24"
4 pieces at 14" x 10 3/4"
2 pieces at 13 1/4" x 13"
2 pieces at 13 1/4" x 10 3/4"
2 pieces at 10 3/4" x 22 1/2"

1/4" Cork
2 pieces at 14" x 24"

8 Wooden Legs (Waddell #2512)

8 Angle Braces (Waddell #2752)

Cubby Credenza . . . page 160

3/4" Birch Veneer Plywood
1 piece at 16" x 48"
2 pieces at 15 3/4" x 48"
4 pieces at 15 3/4" x 24"
3 pieces at 15 3/4" x 15"
1 piece at 14 3/4" x 16 1/2"
1 piece at 14 3/4" x 11 1/2"
1 piece at 14 3/4" x 6 1/4"

1/4" Birch Veneer Plywood
1 piece at 24 3/4" x 48"

3/4" Black Pipe Flanges
4 pieces total

3/4" Threaded Pipe
4 pieces at 6" long

Planter Bench . . . page 198

3/4" Birch Veneer Plywood
1 piece at 18" x 45"
2 pieces at 3" x 45"
3 pieces at 3" x 12"

2" Lattice (1/4" thick)
2 pieces at 18"
2 pieces at 45 1/2"

3/4" Black Pipe Flanges
4 pieces total

3/4" Threaded Pipe
4 pieces at 6" long

3" High Density Foam
1 piece at 27" x 18"

Fabric and Batting:
2 yards fabric
1 yard of 1" thick batting

GLOSSARY

Abstract Art .... Any artistic form that celebrates the representational instead of the realistic.

Backstitch ...... Hand stitch used for making permanent seams or for attaching zippers. Also known as imitation machine stitch.

Bergère .... Upholstered armchair with wood of frame exposed.

Bias .... A 45-degree diagonal to the direction of the weave in a fabric.

Bias Strip .... Strips of material cut from the diagonal of a piece of fabric. Covers piping cord and binds raw edges without bunching.

Binding .... Fabric strip that covers the raw edge of a fabric.

Burlap .... Rough, loosely woven cloth used for upholstery backing.

Credenza .... Sideboard cabinet, usually with metal-grilled doors.

Découpage ...... The art of decorating surfaces with applied paper cutouts sealed under an adhesive.

Double Hem .... Hem in which the fabric is turned over twice, usually by the same amount, so that the raw edge is completely enclosed.

Edge Stitch ..... Line of machine stitching that is as close to the outside edge as possible.

Hem .... Turning under and sewing the raw edge of fabric.

Ladder Stitch ... Used for joining two pieces of patterned fabric, ensuring that the pattern matches across the seam.

Latex Paint ..... Quick-drying, water-based paint suitable for walls and ceiling.

Marquetry ...... Decorative inlay of contrasting woods.

Masking Tape . . . . A low-tack adhesive tape that has multiple decorating uses.

Mitering . . . . Method of neatly turning a hem at a corner.

Monochromatic . . . . Decorative scheme based on one color shifted into multiple varying intensities.

Oil-Based Paint . . . . Slow drying paint suitable for furniture and high traffic areas.

Ottoman . . . . Low upholstered seat or bench having neither back nor arms.

Overlocking . . . . Stitching technique for hiding raw edges.

Patchwork . . . . Method of joining same-sized, or variously sized, pieces of fabric to form larger pieces.

Phillips Head . . . . Type of screw and matching screwdriver with a cross-shaped head.

Pinking . . . . A zigzag cut, often made with pinking shears, to prevent cut edges from unravelling.

Pinning and Tacking . . . Method of securing pieces of fabric together before sewing, either with pins or loose, removable stitches.

Piping . . . . Edging that can be used on most soft furnishings.

Plain Flat Seam . . . . Simplest method of joining two lengths of fabric.

Plumb Line . . . . Cord or string that is secured to a pointed weight and used to ensure straight, vertical lines along walls.

Primer . . . . Liquid substance that is applied to wood or metal before the under coat in order to stabilize the surface.

Raw Edge . . . . Unhemmed, frayed, or cut edge of a piece of fabric.

Running Stitch . . . . Simple stitch that works in and out of layers of fabric, always moving in the same direction.

Seam Allowance . . Amount of material outside of seam, used in joining fabric.

Selvage . . . . Edges of fabric that run down both sides of a length of fabric. These edges are finished off and therefore do not fray.

Slipstitch . . . . Used for hems or where a seam is required along the right side of a fabric, for example when securing closed a cushion cover.

Stenciling . . . . Application of paint over a stencil and onto a surface to produce a design that can be isolated or linked.

Straight Grain . . . Direction of the weave in a fabric.

Studs . . . . Series of small decorative knobs or nailheads. Uprights used in framing of the walls of a building.

Template . . . . Shaped pattern used to cut or sew around an object.

Topstitch . . . . Decorative stitch used to highlight a seam line.

Tufting . . . . The tying down of upholstery by sewing a button through the fabric.

Valance . . . . The top, horizontal part of any drapery arrangement.

Varnish . . . . Substance used for sealing a wooden surface. Available in different glossy finishes and colors.

Velcro . . . . Nylon fastener that consists of two pieces, one with tiny hooks and the other with small loops, which adhere when pressed together.

Veneer . . . . Thin wood or other similar material used to cover the surface of coarse wood to provide a smooth surface.

Warp Threads . . . Lengthwise threads running parallel to a fabric's selvage.

Weft Threads . . . Threads that run across the fabric and over and under the warp threads.

Zigzag Stitch . . . . Machine stitch commonly used to neaten raw edges.

HANDMADE MODERN CAST

TONY LONGORIA

ANN

JASON ROTHENBERG

CONN BRATTAIN

JOSH GEURTSEN

TODD OLDHAM

KELLI HARTLINE

JULIA SZABO

LAUREN SMITH

HILLARY MOORE

DEREK FAGERSTROM

DAVID WISEMAN

JOHN WEIGOLD

BILLY ERB

INDEX

Distinguished as an innovator of accessible design, **Todd Oldham** is the founder of Todd Oldham Studio, a multifaceted, full-service design studio located in New York City. The inspiration for Todd Oldham Studio's designs comes from a celebration of everyday materials and tasks combined with a reverence for sophisticated, refined objects. Todd has made numerous appearances on NBC's *Today* and MTV's *House of Style* and *Crib Crashers*. He is also a photographer whose work has appeared in *L'Uomo Vogue, nest,* and *Interview* magazines. www.toddoldhamstudio.com

Julia Szabo is the author of *Animal House Style* and writes for the *New York Times, New York Post,* and *Country Living.*